The Content Marketing Hurricane

Using Proven Content Marketing Principles to Blow Your Competition Away!

JUSTIN P LAMBERT

DEDICATION

The Content Marketing Hurricane is dedicated to my Reality in Dreams, my wife Melissa, who's felt like she's been in the eye of the hurricane with me for over 15 years now.

Thanks Babe.

CONTENTS

ACKNOWLEDGMENTS

I'd like to take this opportunity to acknowledge those whose expertise has informed and improved my own. For any part you've played in the development of this writer and marketer, this book would never have existed without you:

David Ruzzo	Precision Tax
Scott Carpenter	Carpenter and Associates
Bill Baylis	Online Marketing Muscle
Michael Fern	ContentGems
John Hazard	Contently
Mike White	Urban Shuffle
Debbie Williams	Sprout Content
Dechay Watts	
Andrea Miller	
James Chartrand	Men With Pens
Sonia Simone	Copyblogger Media
Darren Rowse	Problogger
Carol Tice	Make a Living Writing
Woody Stoudemire	Launch Strategic Marketing
Laurie Evans	Gotham LLC
Patrick Westmoreland	X-Factor Web Marketing
Scott Cline	MarketingGhost

INTRODUCTION

Since you're reading this book, I'm going to make a few assumptions about you. (Don't worry, if I'm wrong, you'll still probably enjoy the book, I'll just look like a fool, which is OK.)

Assumption #1: You're either a small business owner, the owner of an underfunded startup, or the person tagged with handling marketing for one or the other.

Assumption #2: You've heard of content marketing before, and probably even have a fair idea what it's all about. But...

Assumption #3: It overwhelms you.

First of all, let me say that you're not alone.

Content marketing is a huge subject, and it's ever evolving. So I'm not surprised if you're overwhelmed.

Let me also be the first "expert" to tell you that there really aren't any true "experts" in the content marketing industry.

Don't get me wrong: there are plenty of knowledgeable folks with lots of experience – I'm proud to count myself in that number – but experts we're not, and here's why:

1. Content marketing covers many different disciplines including search engine optimization, web writing, graphic design, direct response copywriting, marketing analysis, big data, social media, content strategy, social media strategy... the list goes on. Who could possibly be an expert in all of that simultaneously?
2. All of the above has changed dramatically in the last few years, and continues to change every day. That's just the nature of the internet-centric world we all live in now.
3. New tools are being created and perfected as you read this.
4. New rules are being established and broken as you read this, too.
5. The winds of change are blowing at hurricane-level in the marketing world, and have been for a long time now. (Which offers a very nice segue into the theme of this book...)

So I'm not going to try to claim that The Content Marketing Hurricane is going to be your one-stop guide for all things content marketing.

I'm not going to claim you'll achieve overnight content marketing success just by following the principles laid out in this book.

I'm not even going to guarantee you'll achieve content marketing success at all.

But I will promise you this:

Within these pages you will find a step-by-step process that offers you an excellent chance of going from zero to

hero in building your content marketing strategy from scratch, AND content marketing can and will effectively market any product or service you have to offer.

An important note:
It's important to note up front, however, that this book is by no means and all-inclusive guide to starting your own business, or even an all-inclusive marketing guide.

Far from it.

This book focuses solely on building a viable and effective content marketing strategy that can be inserted into your business plan to help you take advantage of the power of content marketing in growing your business.

So, beyond what you learn in these pages, you will also need to handle your other business planning, including (but not limited to) the following:

- Market research
- Legal filings
- Funding and financials
- Developing a conversion funnel
- Developing a high-quality product/service
- Fulfillment
- Customer service
- Plans for growth/expansion
- Etc.

Who is this book for?

I've written this book primarily for the DIY marketer: a brave and hard-working person who is willing to put the time and energy into studying and applying basic content marketing principles in order to develop and maintain a successful content marketing strategy for his business.

Closely related to that guy, is the savvy marketing director or VP who can see some gaps in the way her team is operating and wants to take a "back to basics" approach to shoring up the content marketing process in-house.

Finally, I hope a number of my colleagues read this book too. Why? Because I think a lot of them are doing it wrong. Which is not to say that I'm doing it right, necessarily (see items 1-5 above), but it's my book, so it's my party.

That being said, we're all learning here. So I'd love to improve at all costs, even if that means putting my thoughts out there in concrete form and letting the industry dance all over them.

The formation of a hurricane

To set the stage, let's review why a hurricane is such a perfect metaphor for a successful content marketing strategy.

Disparate Forces
When it first begins to take shape, a hurricane is really just a simple thunderstorm out in the middle of the ocean. No one notices it. It's not accomplishing anything of value. It just... is.

But what's unique about this thunderstorm is that it's formed in the midst of perfect conditions: the air temperature, the water temperature, the prevailing winds, the barometric pressure, all of these disparate forces are ripe to feed off each other.

And so the thunderstorm grows.

Tropical Disturbance

As the exchange of pressure, temperature and moisture continues to intensify, winds pick up and the storm begins spinning slowly around a central eye.

At this point, trained meteorologists who have nothing better to do than to watch the radar screens for this kind of thing notice something's going on out in the ocean. They're certainly not concerned about it yet. But they know it could turn into something, so they keep their eyes on it.

And around this time, the growing storm starts riding the jet stream toward land.

Tropical Depression

The storm continues to grow in speed and intensity.

At this point, any meteorologist who isn't living under a rock knows what's going on and they're even reporting it to viewers at home.

This storm now has a name.

People on the mainland aren't too concerned yet. It's just a bad storm. Some folks who live on islands closer to where it's forming are battening down the hatches, though.

Although it's not too big of a deal yet, it's made a name for itself, and it's starting to provoke action.

Tropical Cyclone (Hurricane)

Speeds have finally reached hurricane level and that tropical depression is about to make landfall. At this point, everyone is taking action: they're boarding up windows, evacuating coastal areas, and it's on their minds even when they're not watching the news!

As the storm works its way toward land, everyone is paying attention and is ready to drop everything and act at a moment's notice.

When it finally makes landfall, well... things will never quite be the same will they?

The formation of a Content Marketing Hurricane

Like a real hurricane, an effective content marketing strategy starts out small and seemingly insignificant. But, with the right combination of "disparate forces" – which we'll discuss in the next section – that strategy starts to build. Each piece of content adds to the building intensity and power of this "storm", and it starts heading toward "land" where the target market resides.

Along the way, with consistent effort, it keeps on picking up steam. First professionals who work in the industry take notice of what's going on, but pretty soon everyone in the target market has to pay attention because this thing's coming right for them!

Finally, when it makes "landfall", that target market absolutely must take action because the combined power of all that strategically planned and skillfully produced content is simply overwhelming.

Conclusion of the introduction
So if you're ready to delve into what makes up a Content Marketing Hurricane, I invite you to turn the page and go for

it!

(If not, and you're already bored, you may as well stop now. It doesn't get any better than this...)

Section One: Disparate Forces

1 WHAT ARE DISPARATE FORCES?

A successful content marketing program needs to consistently offer high-quality content that builds strategically in pursuit of specific goals and a targeted audience. Sporadic explosions of effort here and there are not going to accomplish the purpose, and neither is a constant flow of worthless content.

But that level of commitment, that seemingly endless supply of quality material, and that creative flair that fuels the whole enterprise doesn't just appear out of thin air.

It has to come from somewhere.

As noted in the introduction, the correlation between a successful content marketing program and the formation of a hurricane is striking.

Long before a hurricane hits land, draws attention, or even gets named, it gets its start out in the middle of nowhere as a mixture of "disparate forces" that need to be in the right place at the right time if it's going to have a future ahead of it.

What Disparate Forces create a hurricane?

The two forces every hurricane requires are warm water and moist air. Thunderstorms that drift out over warm water and encounter converging winds are starting to put those forces together.

When warm wet air from the surface of the ocean rises rapidly due to evaporation, then hits cooler air, which makes it condense into storm clouds, conditions are really starting to ripen.

This condensation also releases latent heat, warming the cooler air above the clouds, which in turn makes more room for warm air from the ocean surface to evaporate and rise.

This ongoing cycle of heat exchange and moisture collection, if it goes on long enough without being interrupted, causes the storm to begin spinning around a central, relatively calm, eye.

What Disparate Forces create a Content Marketing Hurricane?

Just as the temperature of the air, the temperature of the water, the amount of available moisture, the prevailing winds, and a number of other factors combine to create the perfect environment for a powerful hurricane, there are certain "disparate forces" that combine to allow for an optimal Content Marketing Hurricane too.

These are:

- **Your upbringing** – what kind of work ethic you were taught, whether or not your creativity was nurtured, how risk adverse your parents were
- **Your background** – the cultural, economic, religious, and social circumstances you grew up in
- **Your circumstances** – your current economic

position, family responsibilities, professional
responsibilities

- **Your unique worldview** – whether you're an optimist
or pessimist, selfish or helpful, committed or easily
bored
- **Your knowledge base** – your level of education, areas
of expertise, your experiences
- **Your desire to learn** – whether you enjoy reading and
study, learning by trial and error, your willingness to
adjust your thinking
- **Your passion** – what truly fires your imagination

All these forces and more combine to make you who you are.

But that's not all.

They also combine to determine what you have to give to the
world. And that's a huge factor in how successful your
Content Marketing Hurricane is going to be.

After all, when you're marketing a product or service with
content, your personality is going to bleed through into the
content you create. As a matter of fact, if it doesn't, you're
doing it wrong because it has to have a strong human element
to touch people.

But I'm getting ahead of myself here.

Let's spend some time breaking down these "disparate forces"
so you can get a full grasp of what each entails.

Exercise #1 – Preparing for Greatness
1. Grab yourself a plain lined notebook and pencil, or if you prefer, your laptop. (Something you can write on

comfortably.)
2. Grab your drink of choice for relaxing contemplation.
3. Read the next chapter.

2 YOUR UPBRINGING

Without getting too Freudian or risking allowing this entire book to collapse into a morass of psychobabble, let's just establish early on that the way you were brought up – whether good, bad, or indifferent – is going to have an impact on your content marketing success.

It's simply common sense: who you are is (at least partly) a product of your upbringing.

So, since marketing a product or service with content is based on the principle of offering people something of value in exchange for their attention, who you are and, by extension, what you have to offer, are important factors.

So, for the next few minutes, take this opportunity to look back at your childhood environment and let's take a look at a few specific areas that where your upbringing shapes your content marketing aptitudes.

(Please note: for the sake of simplicity, in the next few pages as we're discussing the past, I'm going to use the term "parents" as a convenient catch-all for whatever domestic situation you found yourself in as a child. If your particular situation involved foster parents, grandparents, an older sibling, or the nuns at the orphanage, simply insert their names and faces where

appropriate.)

Your work ethic

What kind of attitude did your parents have toward hard work?

Was your Dad the type to hop around from job to job, never really finding his niche? Did he constantly complain about his boss or claim his ship just hadn't come in yet?

Was Mom a workaholic? Never home, or at least never available at home because there was always one more thing that needed to be done?

I'm certainly not passing judgment. No one should, especially if your parents made a conscientious effort to provide for you. But there's no denying that their attitude toward hard work shaped your attitude toward hard work. It's inevitable.

That doesn't mean you're going to think, act, or end up the same as them. Just that you're affected by it.

How so?

If one or both of your parents clearly hated to work hard, you may battle with a tendency toward laziness, procrastination, and a feeling that the world is constantly on your back about something.

If one or both of your parents were workaholics, you may battle with stress, a feeling of inadequacy, and strained relationships because you push yourself too hard.

Even if you've made a conscious effort to think and act

differently from your parents, there's no getting around the psychological impact their example had on you in your formative years.

How does this affect your content marketing?

Marketing with content can be incredibly fun and exciting... sometimes.

It can also be a tremendous amount of work. And let's be honest: sometimes it involves slogging through the busy work just to get it done.

If you were brought up with a balanced, healthy work ethic – viewing hard work as a virtue, enjoying the challenge of setting and reaching meaningful goals, and enjoying the satisfaction that comes with accomplishing something of importance – then you're going to fall in love with content marketing.

But if you're battling negative tendencies – at either extreme of the spectrum – then you're going to struggle with the consistent effort required to effectively build and maintain a successful content marketing strategy.

A strong work ethic will help you take on the inevitable challenges, power through the inevitable slow days, brush yourself off after the inevitable failures, and just generally enjoy the actual work involved in content marketing.

A poor work ethic will turn all those things into potential obstacles that can slow you down or even stop you in your tracks.

Your creativity

If your parents were creative themselves – actors, writers, artists, architects – then they probably brought you up in a creative environment.

If they were office drones and TV addicts, then your creativity may have been stifled somewhat.

Think back: when your parents brought home a surprise from the store, was it a coloring book or a video game? Did they read you a bedtime story, or tell you one they made up? Again, please don't think I'm passing judgment. There's no "right" answer.

However, the extent to which your creativity was nurtured as a child has an impact on your creativity as an adult. Even though the tendency to be more or less creative has a lot to do with natural aptitude, even genetics, your environment plays a role as well.

A recent series of studies conducted at Cornell University and at the National Institute of Psychiatry and Addictions in Budapest made some fascinating discoveries regarding the genetic aspect of creativity.[1]

They found that highly creative people tended to have less of the fibrous bundles of nerves that connect the two hemispheres in the brain (the corpus callosum). The theory is that this more tenuous connection allows each side of their

---

[1]   "Are Some People Born Creative?" by David Cox, The Guardian
      (http://www.theguardian.com/science/blog/2013/sep/19/born-creative-
      study-brain-hemingway)

brain to develop more specialized skills.

Further, researchers at the University of Helsinki noted a particular cluster of genes that was highly developed in people who were particularly creative musically. These genes have been shown to directly affect the brain's plasticity – its ability to forge and maintain new connections.

Interestingly, though, the conclusion of all these studies was aptly summed up this way:

> "So, are we born creative or not? While factors such as upbringing play a crucial role in your brain's development, the work done by scientists in Scandinavia, Germany and the US has shown that having the right genetic makeup can make your brain more inclined towards creative thinking. The rest of us have to "learn" to be creative."

How does this affect your content marketing?

Content marketing is a skill set that fuses both creative and non-creative elements. There are certainly plenty of aspects to a successful content marketing strategy that will make analytical numbers-people jump for joy.

But there's no getting around the fact that creating stellar content requires creative juice. Without it, you'll find your content is dull, dry, and ineffective.

As the researchers noted, while genetics seems to play a large role, and your upbringing is also a huge factor, creativity can also be learned.

So no matter where you fall on the spectrum right now, don't count yourself out. Just be aware and move forward with that knowledge in your back pocket.

Your aversion to risk

If you grew up in very difficult economic circumstances, or in a family that was staunchly conservative, risk-taking probably feels foolish to you.

On the other hand, if you grew up in a hippie compound and your name is Moonbeam, you may not think twice about striking off on something new.

If you think back, you can no doubt hear your Mom yelling at you from the back door to get out of that tree because "you're gonna break your neck!"

Or, maybe you can think back and see your Dad handing you your very first BB gun at the tender age of 9, and showing you how to use it to keep the squirrels away from the bird feeder.

You may have experienced a major upheaval – a parent's job loss, an unexpected medical bill, losing a home, or a divorce – that changed your attitude toward risk-taking.

Whatever the case may be, the extent to which you're willing to put yourself, your family, your finances, and your reputation at risk has a lot to do with how risk was handled at home when you were a kid.

How does this affect your content marketing?

The optimal attitude toward risk for a content marketer lies somewhere between the two extremes noted above. Since successful content marketing requires the development and following of a quality content strategy, there's some conservative thought surrounding that. But, to make this strategy effective, it needs to push the envelope a little bit, even take some risks.

The balance here is that they are calculated risks, and they're tested for efficacy as the strategy progresses.

If you're completely risk adverse, you'll have a difficult time putting yourself out there like you need to when you're marketing with content.

On the other hand, if you don't even know the meaning of the word risk, you could very well stray off-strategy with ill-advised forays into crazy.

Neither is going to move your Content Marketing Hurricane toward land.

So now what?

It probably seems like we're starting things out on a negative footing, but that's not the case.

Few people can look back at the perfect upbringing. I know I can't. Neither can my kids, for that matter.

But here's the important thing: none of what we've discussed in this chapter involves prophecy or rules that are set in stone.

Far from it.

Rather, this has been about awareness.

If you're aware of the impact your upbringing has on your

ability and aptitude to effectively create and distribute quality content, you can work within your personal parameters and make magic happen.

Remember, the thunderstorm that forms out over the ocean has no control over the temperature of the water or the moisture in the air. But it can use them to its own advantage.

Exercise #2 – Brainstorming: Your Upbringing
1. Think back to how you were brought up – the examples that were set for you, the lessons you learned, the things you wish you could change.   2. On paper, brainstorm a list of words and phrases that come to mind as you think about your work ethic, your creativity, and your feelings about risk. (Don't edit yourself here. There are no right or wrong answers, this is just a means of getting something concrete out of letting your mind wander.)   3. When you're done, don't even read it. Go to the next chapter.

3 YOUR BACKGROUND

Now we'll take a slightly broader view, outside your home life and into the larger picture of your background.

For many of the same reasons your upbringing has an impact on your chances for content marketing success, your background does too. In some cases, the effect is even more profound.

To put a frame around the discussion, I'm breaking down your background into four major categories:

- Cultural
- Religious
- Economic
- Social

As we discuss each, I want to make sure I'm clearly understood: absolutely nothing about your background makes you automatically more or less likely to succeed in content marketing. And certainly nothing about it creates a liability you'll need to disguise or compensate for.

On the contrary, nearly everything about your background can be made an asset in your efforts to create and distribute stellar content. But that will only be the case if you're aware of how your background affects the way you perceive the world, and the way the world perceives you.

Cultural background

The culture you grew up in has shaped your view of those who share your culture and those who fall outside that sphere.

This has been proven by numerous studies. One that grabbed my attention was done a few years back at the University of Michigan[1] where researchers noted the differences between European Americans and Asian Americans in regards to how they judge another person's personality.

The study found that European Americans tended to judge based on specific actions they observed while Asian Americans tended to judge based on a broader contextual view.

The researchers noted:

> "European American culture emphasizes individual independence; meanwhile, Asian culture is more interdependent and more sensitive to social contexts. This difference means European Americans are inclined to account for someone's behavior by making assumptions about their personality, while Asians are not (at least not without some context.)"

---

[1]   "Culture Influences Judgment of Others" by Wynne Perry, LiveScience.com (http://www.livescience.com/13700-personality-traits-culture-independence-social-context.html)

Psychologist and neuroscientist Merlin Donald noted the following in his book, A Mind So Rare[2]:

> "Symbolizing cultures own a direct path into our brains and affect the way major parts of the executive brain become wired up during development. This is the key idea behind the notion of deep enculturation."

Obviously, some people could use this information to try to claim some sort of superiority or inferiority of various cultures. But nothing could be further from the truth.

Albert Camus made an interesting point in his book, Lyrical and Critical Essays[3]:

> "Men express themselves in harmony with their land. And superiority, as far as culture is concerned, lies in this harmony and nothing else. There are no higher or lower cultures. There are cultures that are more or less true."

So, while different cultures inevitably lead to differences in how people view each other and the world around them, they have no bearing at all on superiority or inferiority.

Rather, embracing cultural diversity and cultivating an appreciation for the cultures of others enhances your own worldview and your appeal to others.

2 "A Mind So Rare" by Merlin Donald, 2001, W.W. Norton & Co., pg. 212

3 "Lyrical and Critical Essays" by Albert Camus, 1970, Vintage. (As reported in "How Important is Culture in Shaping Our Behavior?" by David Vogner, Huffington Post (http://www.huffingtonpost.com/david-vognar/culture-influence-politics-life-_b_1724750.html)

Religious background

In much the same way as culture, your religious background (or lack thereof) is going to alter the lens through which you see the world.

Various religions tend toward certain emotional hot buttons that a background steeped in religious instruction can bring to the fore.

For example, for Catholics, guilt is a prime emotional trigger.

For Buddhists, peace and enlightenment are major drivers.

Atheists tend to focus on analytical logic and rationality while Pentecostals rely heavily on faith and the "movement of the Spirit."

What becomes clear as you think about your own religious background is that it shapes far more than just your belief in a higher power. It shapes your attitude toward such overarching concepts as good and evil, right and wrong, morals, ethics, and human rights.

Like religion itself, these are big topics that reach uncomfortably into the core of who we are as people, and into how we interact with our fellow humans.

So naturally, your religious background is going to either consciously or subconsciously affect anything you create.

Economic background

Whether you grew up rich or poor, money was likely a powerful force in your life.

Note the comments of child psychologist, Robert Coles[4]:

> "At an early age, children sort themselves out as belonging to this or that aspect of race, neighborhood, et cetera, and this sorting is very much connected to money. Their conclusions are generally based on what their parents can offer them and what dangers still remain in their lives."

If you grew up in a home with very little money, barely scraping by, or not quite, then you likely have a keen understanding of the value of budgeting, saving, conserving and finding value in the basics.

On the other hand, if you grew up in an affluent environment, you may have been exposed to an array of experiences in the fields of travel, education, and entertainment, for instance. These experiences form a background that someone with less financial resources in their past likely does not possess.

Again, there's no right or wrong, better or worse situation here. Both extremes of economic circumstances produce positive and negative effects, all of which can be enhanced or counteracted by simple common sense and conscious

---

4   "How Does Wealth Affect Children? A Conversation With Robert Coles" by Pamela Gerloff, More Than Money, (http://www.morethanmoney.org/articles.php?article=How_Does_Wealth_ Affect_Children_278)

reasoning.

But the impressions, memories, and emotional impact they leave behind are indelible. You can either ignore them, or use them to your advantage.

Social background

Although often tied closely with the cultural, religious, and economic backgrounds already discussed, your social background does bring some unique characteristics to the table that warrant some brief comments.

For the sake of this discussion, we'll call your social background the way you learned to interact with others.

Were you raised with a strong sense of community? Were you interested in what was going on with your neighbors? Did your parents go to town meetings or join the PTA?

Then you've likely carried that social tendency forward into your own life. You've probably developed an interdependent attitude, establishing your place in your local community, your job, or your industry, and working naturally to strengthen that position by working with others.

On the other hand, were you isolated as a child, whether due to circumstances or a parent's personality?

Then you're probably very independent by nature. Maybe you're socially awkward, or you've worked hard to overcome that.

Your social background could also affect whether you inherently trust others or if you're leery of them. Are other people here to add color and joy to your life, or are they just here to get in the way?

Certainly, we can learn to overcome social taboos and introverts can develop the ability to at least *seem* outgoing, but our social background still leaves permanent imprints on who we are.

How does this affect your content marketing?

All this talk of religion and culture might have felt a bit deep and left-field in a book about content marketing, but I assure you, it's not.

In all these areas, your background is going to have a bearing on your unique perspective – the lens through which you see the world – as well as others' view of you.

It's not always pretty, and it's not always fair. But it is simple human nature. We tend to think of people, places, things and situations in ways that were dictated by our background in relation to them.

For example, consider the potentially controversial subject of gun ownership.

If you grew up in a culture that historically supported owning a gun – such as the American south, for instance – you're going to think about the gun debate a lot differently than someone who grew up in a culture where guns were anathema, like the suburbs of London.

If your religious convictions are so strong that the idea of even potentially harming someone is morally repugnant to you, the chance of your choosing to own a gun for personal defense is slim. Whereas if your religious background is not that strict, or doesn't view self-defense as equivalent to murder, then you won't have the same moral barrier to cross.

Economical and social factors come into the mix as well, affecting how you feel – deep inside – about matters, and how willing you are to change that belief based on changes in your environment or your knowledge.

All of these effects will clearly shine through in the content you create if you're producing content with the level of passion and transparency that's necessary for long-term success. They will be infused in your voice, the tone you use when discussing certain subjects, the conviction with which you debate your arguments, the finesse with which you polish your prose.

And it will draw some people to you like flies to honey, while it will inevitably push others away.

That's OK. That's part of the magic of The Content Marketing Hurricane.

Exercise #3 – Brainstorming: Your Background
1. Consider your own cultural, religious, economic, and social background.
2. Write down any words or phrases that come to mind as you think about these aspects of your past. Concentrate specifically on what kinds of feelings your memories evoke. (Again, don't edit yourself. This is just exploration right now.)
3. If you were forced to defend your views on cultural, religious, social or economic topics, how would you feel about doing so?

4. Read the next chapter.

4 YOUR CIRCUMSTANCES

Let's move our discussion up a few years and talk about what's happening with you *right now*.

Your personal, economic, and family circumstances will profoundly affect your content marketing success. Let's take a glance at each of these in turn, then discuss how they affect the creation of your Content Marketing Hurricane.

Personal circumstances

The age-old axiom states, "Life is 10% what happens to you and 90% how you react to it."

While that's certainly true, that 10% can be a powerful force.

Just consider a few examples of personal circumstances that can have a huge impact on your life.

- Your health
- Where you live
- Where you work
- What you do in your free time

All of these areas could easily slip right under your radar... until something serious happens:

- You get seriously ill
- Your apartment building gets sold or you're evicted.
- You lose your job
- You take up pole-dancing for cash

You see, for obvious reasons your current personal circumstances have a direct impact on how you feel, how you interact with others, your level of stress, and your ability to create.

How does this affect your content marketing?

Your personal circumstances directly impact your supply of the most important resources you can give to a content marketing program: time and effort.

If your personal circumstances are such that, with a little maneuvering, you can set aside a few hours a day to dedicate to creating and distributing content, you're going to be in a prime position to make a go of this endeavor.

If you can only dedicate a few minutes a day, you can still make positive strides, but you need to realistically understand that it's going to be slow-going for a while.

And if you simply can't afford to spend any time or effort on creating or distributing content... well, then you may as well stop reading right here, at least until your circumstances change a bit.

Don't worry, I'll be right here when you come back.

Economic circumstances

Just as your economic background left an indelible impact on your psyche, your current economic circumstances can and will do the same.

If you are currently struggling with money problems, you're probably stressed. Your time is being absorbed by working extra hours or looking for more work. Your relationships may be suffering for either or both of these reasons.

Strangely enough, people who are very wealthy will sometimes fall into the same trap: to maintain their lifestyle or continue to grow their wealth, they end up working too much, neglecting their health or family responsibilities, and succumbing to stress.

These are just rash generalizations, of course, because many affluent people lead very balanced and healthy lives, and many people with little materially still maintain positive and productive outlooks.

But the fact remains that your economic circumstances will likely have an effect on what you can dedicate toward new projects.

How does this affect your content marketing?

Your economic circumstances will have a direct impact on how much time, money, and energy you can invest in a content marketing program.

Being short on funds causes stress, and makes you feel desperate. You can make poor decisions and rush to take action without thinking it through appropriately.

On the other hand, financial stability offers a foundation on which to base well-planned strategy and calculated risk. It allows you to take a longer view of the future instead of focusing strictly on short-term turnaround.

Content marketing is a long-term strategy that will not provide instant overnight success. While it can, theoretically, begin generating leads from the outset, it is far more likely to receive almost no response as it first begins to coalesce. After all, it's still out over the ocean in the middle of nowhere, and it hasn't built up any steam yet. No one's paying attention.

If you're currently working a job and considering starting a business in the future, start building your Content Marketing Hurricane now while you have reliable income so you can concentrate on creating the best strategically viable content without worrying about ROI at the beginning.

If you are currently running a business and are desperate for leads and paying customers to cover next month's operating expenses, it may not be the best time to start a content marketing program.

Or, if you have the discipline to do so, you can start working on the program without looking at it as a source of income at all. Simply add it to your daily administrative tasks that do not fall under billable time and leave it at that until it starts producing fruit.

If you can adjust your economic circumstances for the better without derailing your content marketing program, absolutely do it. The more stability you have going in, the faster your Content Marketing Hurricane will gain momentum, and the stronger it will become.

Family circumstances

While closely connected to personal and economic circumstances, the family demands a few moments on its own for the simple fact that if you have a spouse and/or children relying on you, your time and energy is necessarily divided. They must come first if there's a conflict, and their needs and desires have to be on your mind as you're planning any adjustments to your routine (such as implementing a content marketing strategy.)

How does this affect your content marketing?

Content marketing is a time-consuming effort, and it requires persistence and commitment over a long period.

If your family commitments are such that doing so will hurt one or more family member, not only are you morally obligated to adjust your priorities, you're also unlikely to be able to put your all into whatever effort you can muster.

In every way, it becomes a losing proposition.

Of course, people of every walk of life are making a success of content marketing, so I'm certainly not implying that, say, a single mother of two who puts together a powerful Content Marketing Hurricane is somehow neglecting her responsibilities. Or that a husband who does so has, by definition, neglected his wife.

On the contrary, these individuals have likely learned how to effectively adjust their priorities to the extent that their family responsibilities are fully cared for while also allowing for dedication to building the content marketing program. This is not impossible by any means.

But it also doesn't come automatically. It requires concerted effort.

Of course, anything worth doing takes effort, right?

Exercise #4 – Brainstorming: Your Circumstances
1. Think about your personal, family, and economic circumstances as they are right now.
2. Write down pros and cons of your current circumstances.
3. Write down ideas as they come to you that could lessen the cons and accentuate the pros.
4. Read the next chapter.

5 YOUR UNIQUE WORLDVIEW

It's as unique to you as your fingerprint, and its impossible for anyone else to perfectly imitate.

What is it?

Your unique worldview – the way you see the world and your own place in it.

Your worldview involves aspects of your personality as well as your emotional connection to your environment and the people who inhabit it.

It's formed – at least in part – by a combination of forces we've already discussed like your upbringing and your background, but it's one force you have a lot of conscious control over as well.

As noted in one of the Core Tenets of The Worldview Exploration Project created by the Institute for Noetic Sciences[5],

> "Worldviews not only impact how we
> understand and make sense of the world

---

5   "The Worldview Explorations Project Core Tenets", Institute of Noetic Sciences, (http://noetic.org/education/worldview/tenets/)

```
around us but also influence how we
express ourselves in the world. The
constellation of personal values,
beliefs, assumptions, attitudes, and
ideas that make up our worldview have an
affect on our goals and desires,
relationships and behaviors. The more
aware we become of our worldview and the
worldviews of others, the more
effectively we can navigate through
life."
```

For example, based on your background and upbringing, you may tend to be an optimist, or a pessimist. You may lean toward being altruistic and helpful, or selfish. You may be able to readily commit yourself to a cause or a project, or you may be easily bored and restless.

Your level self-esteem, your personal inhibitions, and even your secret prejudices, all play a role in shaping your worldview, and all can be traced back to some aspect of your background or upbringing.

But in all these cases, unlike cultural or economic forces that changed who you were as your brain was developing, these aspects of your personality are yours to play with.

Despite your natural inclination, you can choose to be more positive, more generous, more goal-oriented. Regardless of what your parents did or didn't do, you can choose to value yourself, to make smart choices, and to favor equality.

Your worldview is yours to create, not simply a product of your past that you have no control over.

How does this affect your content marketing?

There are a million different variations on this theme: what you've come from has combined to color your perspective on the world in a way that's unique to you. And that perspective, in turn, colors everything you think, do, say... or create.

As in, content.

So, the point here is not just to try to change who you are or how you view the world. It's not about trying to put that integral part of you into the background while you're creating content so you can write or record something that you think is "more appropriate" or "politically correct".

On the contrary!

This is about being aware of how your unique worldview is going to affect what you create, and using that knowledge to your advantage! Because your unique worldview is the basis of one of the most important ingredients you can add to this developing storm: your voice.

And as we'll discuss in more depth in a later section, your unique voice is integral to creating engaging content that truly speaks to your target audience.

Exercise #5 – Brainstorming: Your Unique Worldview
1. Consider how your viewpoint differs from other people you know.
2. In five sentences or less, describe that worldview as if writing to someone who has never met you.
3. Read the next chapter.

6 YOUR KNOWLEDGE BASE

You might notice that I used the term "knowledge base" for this chapter rather than "education", and there's an important reason for making that distinction.

I don't feel that your level of education has much if any impact on your potential success in content marketing.

Granted, if you can't read or write, you're going to struggle, and you'll probably fail. That's just life. Sorry if that seems harsh, but it's a fact. (My only saving grace is that if you can't read, you're not being offended by this right now, because it's in print.)

But, beyond the bare minimum basics of reading, writing, arithmetic and life skills, no degree is going to give you a leg up in reaching content marketing success.

But, your knowledge base – what you've learned through study, through trial and error, and through passive experience – is a completely different story.

Most people tend to downplay their knowledge. After all, if you seem to know too much, you're stuck up. Of course, if you know too little, you're stupid.

We feel pretty safe in the middle: "I know enough to get by, but that's about it."

But the fact is, there are probably a few subjects in which you truly excel. These are the topics your friends and family always call you about because they know you'll know the answer. These are the categories you run through in Jeopardy to the frustrated stares of your spouse. These are those "secret guilty pleasures" you actually occasionally Google just for the fun of it because you enjoy keeping up with the topic.

And there s nothing wrong with that at all.

How does this affect your content marketing?

The fact is, deep knowledge in one or more fields can be gold to a content marketer, because it means you won't need to dig so hard for valuable information to share with others who want to learn about that subject.

Now, of course, it's not realistic to assume that whatever you know a lot about is going to be the exact niche you're going to make a killing in when your Content Marketing Hurricane makes landfall. There are only so many books and videos you can make about Hungarian Clog dancing, after all.

But, the real question is this: how can what you already know be used strategically to make your content more interesting, more appealing, or more exciting?

Is there a gimmick there? A metaphor you can use? A natural connection you can exploit to bring your subject into the conversation and really give people something to think about?

(Hint: I've always been fascinated by the weather. Not enough to actually become a meteorologist, mind you, but just enough to realize that a hurricane made a fantastic metaphor for carrying out a killer content marketing strategy. See where I'm going here?)

So don't downplay your knowledge. On the contrary, play it up. Make it work for you.

Exercise #6 – Brainstorming – Your Knowledge Base
1. Think about what subjects you already know like the back of your hand, and write as extensive a list of these as you can. 2. Once you finish the list, go back and immediately cross off anything that irritates you. (We all know more than we'd like about some things.) 3. If it doesn't immediately annoy you, leave it. We'll come back to it later. 4. Read the next chapter.

7 YOUR DESIRE TO LEARN

If money and time were non-factors, what would you absolutely love to learn about?

Taking a step further back, how do you feel about learning in general?

If you're anything like me, you look back at the years you spent in school and kick yourself hard when you realize how much of that time you squandered goofing off or complaining when all anyone ever wanted you to do was *learn things*. What I wouldn't give for the opportunity to sit in a classroom for several hours a day every day – FOR FREE! - and just enjoy the process of taking in and assimilating knowledge.

But not everyone feels that way about learning. For some people, reading, studying, and trying to retain information is daunting and difficult.

Some people hate it.

Others can't stand learning by trial and error. They want to get it right the first time every time, so they spend a lot of time with books and strategies trying to work everything out to the T, sometimes even getting stuck in "analysis paralysis".

But life is messy, and it's constantly changing the rules of the game on us as we go.

So this goes far beyond academics. Your willingness and ability to learn is really a measure of your willingness and ability to grow.

What do you want to be when you grow up?

We've all been asked that question as kids, and we all had the greatest answers: a fireman, an astronaut, the President...
All really ambitious goals, especially for five-year old kids who couldn't even spell "president" yet.

Then, as we got older, we started learning and developing. We built up impressive sets of skills and a backlog of experience. We did the best we could to apply ourselves so we could finally graduate and become...

What?

An entry-level clerk in a cubicle? A middle manager in a corporate jungle?

Dissatisfied?

Bored?

What happened?

What happened to our dreams? Our impressive goals for our future? Why do so many of us settle for ho-hum when we shot for heroic as kids?

Not to say that an entry-level position is a bad thing at all. Or middle management, for that matter (although from personal experience, I have to say middle management has its suck-factor.)

Sometimes a job is a job to pay the bills. A step toward something else, or a rung on a ladder.

But the problem comes in when you get to the bottom rung on the ladder and you stop climbing.

This applies to a lot more than your secular career too.

Have you stopped learning? Stopped growing as a person? Have you given up changing?

Be a tree, not a wall.

Sometimes I think man's ability to build and create so many things has clouded our understanding of nature. Think about this:

When a man builds a wall, it's a finished thing. He places brick on brick, spreading mortar in-between, and once it's all lined up and in place, he stops. The wall hardens and it serves its purpose until time and circumstance see fit to destroy it.

A brick wall doesn't grow. It doesn't adapt. It just is.

And that's fine for a brick wall. But what about you?

Instead, think of a tree.

A tree can live for thousands of years. And during that entire time, what is it doing?

It's growing. Pushing new leaves out of old branches every year. expanding its trunk, shoving roots down into soil seeking nutrients and water, thickening its bark and pushing ever taller.

A growing tree adapts to circumstances, sometimes growing sideways to get to the light, sometimes breaking concrete to get to the soil underneath...

Or destroying a brick wall if necessary.

That's life in nature. Life never settles. Life never reaches a point where development stops.

Do you know what that's called? When life stops growing and changing?

It's called death.

How ambitious are you?

So what's it going to be?

Life or death?

I know, it probably sounds melodramatic, but seriously. If you stop growing, you're really dying in a fundamental way.

So how ambitious are you?

How willing are you to look beyond the next minute, the next hour, the next day, and start really taking a good long look at where your life is heading?

Do you have any long-term goals on the horizon? Anything of

value to shoot for?

Do you have any plans in mind as to how you're going to get where you want to go?

Are you prepared to make the changes necessary to improve your life? To meet the people you need to meet? To do the things you need to do?

Because change is always going to be necessary. You're going to need to adapt to what life throws at you if you're going to grow.

And it isn't going to be easy.

How easy do you think it is for a tree root to break concrete?

But it happens. Every day.

That's because the root is ambitious by nature, and persistent. And it's not afraid to work hard.

What about you?

How does this affect your content marketing?

OK, I'm back down off my soapbox for a bit, sorry about that.

If you're hoping to create and grow a Content Marketing Hurricane, your attitude toward learning in general, and learning about your chosen topic(s) specifically are going to have a huge impact on how successful you are.

Content marketing is an evolving field based to a large extent around the fact that you can never finish learning. For that reason, someone who is dead set against learning new things, new ways of operating, and new methods of success is not going to make it in content marketing. They're simply not a good fit.

That doesn't mean that success in content marketing has any specific connection to your IQ or your level of book smarts. And as we already noted, it's not connected to a degree or level of formal schooling either.

Rather, it has to do with your *willingness and desire* to learn and, by extension, to help others to do so.

Exercise #7 – Brainstorming: Your Willingness to Learn

1. Imagine you were given a free pass to attend every High School or College class, seminar, webinar, and correspondence course ever devised.
2. Write a list of all the classes you would attend, and include a brief explanation of what you'd hope to gain from that course.
3. Now, pick your absolute favorite from that list, go to Google and search "free courses _____" with your choice in the blank space.
4. Learn something.
5. Read the next chapter.

---

8 YOUR PASSION

If there's any word that's truly been overused in the area of content marketing (and there are probably hundreds) it's **passion**.

Allow me to offer a few synonyms so we can all stop relying so heavily on buzzwords:

- fervor
- ardor
- enthusiasm
- eagerness
- zeal
- vigor
- fire
- energy
- fervency
- animation
- spirit
- fanaticism

You get the point.

I think a lot of people misuse the term – even the whole concept of – passion. They use it as if it s synonymous with interest or niche.

But it's not.

Let's get this straight: you can't form a passion based on what subject you determine to be profitable.

Likewise, you can't automatically make your true passions profitable. There are going to be some things that truly fire your imagination that no one else cares about.

But, that's not going to be the case with all of them.

And where your real passions – those topics you can't stop talking about, those items that keep you giddy with anticipation – intersect with the passions of others, there you begin to feel the force that will help form your Hurricane.

A few words about hard work

I'm hopping back up on my soapbox for a few minutes, because this is a subject that irritates me. If you'd like to skip ahead to the "how does this affect your content marketing" section, you'll see where I'm going with this rant.

Few things are more highly praised and more energetically avoided than hard work.

Ask anyone if they'd like their son or daughter to grow up fat, lazy and spoiled. What do you think they'll say?

Of course not! What a horrible thought!

And yet, ironically, that's exactly what we seem to be encouraging them to do!

Maybe not in word, per se, but in attitude and in example, absolutely!

(Warning: Here comes the hypocritical advice!)

Hypocritical Advice

I do this too, so forgive me for pointing this out. If it feels better, consider it more of a common sense voice coming from behind you somewhere in the crowd:

Especially in the United States, we seem to have this inborn aversion to hard work. I'm sure it's spreading all over the developed world, of course, because all the worst traits do.

For example, consider potential careers for a moment.

Would you prefer to be (or to help your children become) a ditch digger or a computer programmer? An auto mechanic or a lawyer? A farmer or a CEO? A mason or a writer?

(Alright, granted, no one wants their kid to grow up to be a writer.)

But you get the point.

For reasons that have little or nothing to do with common sense, logic, or the relative value of the work being accomplished, we automatically gravitate to the white collar desk job being somehow better than the blue collar labor job.

If a kid considers dropping out of High School or skipping college, we threaten them with something like, "what do you want to do, dig ditches for the rest of your life?"

Not that I'm advocating dropping out of school, but what the heck's wrong with digging ditches?

And, to a large extent, salaries reflect that attitude as well. While we might think it's outrageous what a mechanic might charge us to fix our car, it's absolutely NOTHING compared to what a lawyer will charge us to write a few letters and file a form.

And compare the amount of actual WORK required by each!Who's actually earning that money?

Now before you jump up and down on that last comment, I'm not trying to say that lawyers, accountants, or even writers for that matter, aren't worth their pay.

They absolutely are.

All I'm saying is that those folks who actually break a sweat doing what they do are notoriously under-appreciated and under-paid considering the effort they need to put in.

Now think about what your life would be like if there were no ditch diggers, mechanics, plumbers, carpenters, bricklayers, pavers, farmers, long-haul truckers, janitors, maintenance workers, window washers, sanitary workers, landscapers, not to mention the thousands of other manual labor jobs I've left out.

It would be a really messy, chaotic and unpleasant world where none of our incredible machines could save us from the nasty underbelly of life.

Sad but true.

Can we change our attitude?

So can we change our attitude toward hard work?

Well, yes and no.

As a society, humans have always viewed "progress" as the movement from hard work to less hard work:

Technology is created to make it possible for us to accomplish more with the same amount of work, or to accomplish the same with less work.

The building of wealth allows one to progress from working hard to paying others to work hard for you.

Improved education allows you to qualify for the "better" jobs that don't require you to work hard. At least not with your body.

Is this always bad?

No. Technology, wealth and education are all tools that can vastly improve our lives, and if they're used properly, no one can argue that they hurt us more than they help. So, as a society, it's tough to imagine our overall attitude changing on that score.

But, individually, we certainly can change the way we view hard work for ourselves, and the way we view those who work hard for a living.

The joy of hard work

Never underestimate the joy and contentment you can find in working hard.

I know personally, I hate the *thought* of mowing my lawn. I have a pretty big lawn for my neighborhood. Right around an acre. Plus it's all hill, and there are about three thousand obstructions in the way of the mower.

And it's a push-mower. Not a rider, not a walk-behind, but a push mower.

So it's a lot of work, and I absolutely hate the *thought* of doing it.

But once I actually muscle through and get it done, my body gives me the old "well done" and I tamp that down with a cold beer. Then I look out at my gorgeous lawn, smell the awesome scent of newly-cut grass, and I feel a level of satisfaction I don't get out of many other activities.

It's a really powerful force, and one that a lot of athletes, artists, mechanics and other professionals who work with their hands understand:

"I did this. This is here because of me."

Hard work just plain feels good.

So give it a try in your own life. The next time you're considering a home improvement project or some clean-up in the yard, instead of hopping online and starting to compare quotes from contractors to come do it for you, why not hop online for how-to information so you can roll up your sleeves and give it a try?

And if your son or daughter has a real affinity for working with their hands, and doesn't mind getting them dirty, don't be too quick to laugh off their thoughts of fixing cars or building houses for a living. After all, someone has to fix cars and build houses. A quality mechanic or construction contractor is going to make a nice, solid living doing it. And if they truly love their job, where's the down side?

OK, I'm coming back down. But before I do, there's one more topic to cover. Again, if you'd like to skip ahead, you'll see how this all pans out.

A few words about persistence

Have you ever noticed that everyone seems to be capable of starting major, ground-breaking, world-changing projects? The thing is, only a rare few manage to finish them. And we call those people geniuses, leaders and heroes.

"Genius is 1% inspiration and 99% perspiration." ~ Thomas Edison

Unfortunately, just like so many other negative traits we wish we could kick to the curb, the tendency to tire out on an idea, lose steam on a project, or crumble when we run into obstacles, is human nature. It's common to nearly every man, woman and child in the world, and it's not going to be an easy habit to break.

But, it's definitely possible. And here's how:

Think big

First, if you are considering a project, a solution to a problem you're facing, or any other significant action, don't limit yourself to the bare-bones minimum. It's tough to get excited about "enough to get by." It's easy, though, to get excited about "bigger and better than ever before!"

So start big, and work your way down to "okay" as you go. The worst that could happen is that you end up with a solution or finished project that meets your needs. And the bonus is that you learned a ton about what's possible along the way, which makes you more apt to shoot even higher next time!

Prepare for the worst, but aim for the best

This may sound trite, but it's important. By preparing for the worst, you free yourself from worrying about it, and you can see clearly how it may come to be. This allows you to focus your energies and efforts on avoiding it.

That way, your aim remains on the more positive target and you're more likely to keep shooting for it because worry and fear won't slow you down.

Treat obstacles as hurdles, not brick walls

When a runner is sprinting down the track, eyes on the finish line, peripheral vision noting the fact that his fellow runners are keeping up with him neck-and-neck, he barely sees each hurdle he needs to jump.

Sure, he knows they're there. He has to make an effort to get over them. But a trained runner with his eyes on victory doesn't even break stride when a hurdle gets in the way.

Imagine, though, if that same runner suddenly sees a ten-foot-high brick wall loom up in his lane. You'd better believe he'll be slowing down, probably even stopping. It's intimidating and potentially dangerous.

And that's exactly why you need to view the inevitable obstacles that get in the way of every project or goal you start as hurdles rather than walls. That means realizing they're there and putting the effort necessary into clearing them, but not allowing it to break your stride.

This is easier said than done, of course, but it's certainly not impossible. Success relies primarily on your state-of-mind, (just like competitive running,) and realizing that very few obstacles are actually as bad as they look or sound at the outset. Most, in fact, are tiny and hardly worth your concern.

Just do it

Sorry, Nike. But really, that's all that's left to this subject.

Persistence, when it's all said and done, comes down to just putting your head down and muscling through whatever it is you want or need to do. I put this step last, of course, because it's the most difficult and accomplishing the prior steps should make it easier.

But even after you take the time and effort to think big, plan ahead for the best outcome, prepare for all contingencies and maintain the right perspective on your obstacles, you're still going to have to dig down deep for the mental, emotional and physical strength to keep on going.

Which – if you've stuck with me this long, you've probably guessed – is where passion comes in.

How does this affect your content marketing?

Whatever it is, it fires your imagination. It brings a smile to your face. And – perhaps most importantly for our discussion – it has *staying power*.

See, if you're passionate about something, you're in a position to stick with it through the inevitable tough times that come to any content marketer: the days when writing another blog post feels like a trip up Sisyphus' mountain. When an infographic you poured your soul into garners three retweets. When "that other blog" suddenly launches a brand new e-book that looks a heck of a lot like the one you've been building to launch next week.

If you have passion for your topic, your industry, your point of view... none of that matters. You're going to keep going.

And taking a strategy from "disparate forces" right on through to "landfall" requires that kind of hard work and persistence.

Exercise #8 – Brainstorming: Your Passion
1. Explore your attitude toward hard work and persistence. Specifically, what subjects, projects, or goals give you the push you need to excel?
2. Look back to your other lists and circle any items that are repeated on this list.
3. Read the next chapter.

9 PULLING TOGETHER YOUR DISPARATE FORCES

If you've read this far and you've nodded your head at least a few times, you probably have a fairly good understanding of how your upbringing, your background, and all the other "disparate forces" we've discussed can work together to drive your Content Marketing Hurricane.

Of course, these are factors that everyone has available to them to some extent. But not everyone is going to make a success of content marketing. The real magic happens where all these forces intersect under the right conditions.

Once you have given real thought to each of these areas, and you've truly identified the aspects of each that will be affecting your content, brainstorming (no pun intended) should result in a handful of clear intersection points where you either already know or want to learn enough about something and are passionate enough about it that you can succeed at marketing it to the world.

The potential for intersections is basically endless, so I won't belabor the point here with a bunch of examples. Suffice to say, you'll know them when you see them. They'll jump out at you as seemingly obvious "a-ha" revelations.

These points of intersection will form the basis of your most successful content marketing efforts.

That doesn't mean that you can't possibly succeed marketing products or services that fall outside these areas. As a matter of fact, a lot of professionals are able to successfully market just about anything, whether it floats their boat or not. (I like to count myself among them.)

But if you do focus on a topic that comes out of this brainstorm, it's going to be a heck of a lot easier.

And it's going to be fun.

Moving forward

With all that in mind, we're ready to start moving out of the realm of theory and into actual practice.

Looking back at that storm forming out in the middle of the ocean, those disparate forces – the water temperature, the air temperature, humidity, pressure, wind – have met in the right conditions to start feeding off each other and gaining strength.
Now, it's building to the point that it starts to coalesce into something of substance. The clouds have stacked miles high, the wind is picking up, and pretty soon, it's going to start spinning around a central eye.

Your Content Marketing Hurricane has reached the Tropical Disturbance stage.

Exercise #9 – Brainstorming: Intersections
1.   Review all your notes from the last seven exercises

2. Note where topics fell off the list, and where new ideas surfaced.
3. Note where strengths (in what you know, what you love to learn about, and what you're passionate about) become obvious.
4. These points of intersection will become the focus of the next step in building your Content Marketing Hurricane.
5. Read the next chapter.

Section Two: Tropical Disturbance

10 WHAT IS A TROPICAL DISTURBANCE?

Now that we've discussed all the "disparate forces" that combine to form the optimal conditions for your Content Marketing Hurricane, let's assume you've found your points of intersection and your storm is starting to gain power and to move toward land.

You've reached the stage meteorologists call, "tropical disturbance".

Basically, once the storm begins building power from the exchange of heat and moisture from the ocean and the atmosphere, that power is released in the form of wind and rain. Once the wind picks up to a fast enough clip and the pressure exchange is regular enough, the storm begins to spin around a central eye, creating the famous whirlpool appearance that marks a gathering hurricane.

Now at this point, meteorologists are starting to take notice. It's nothing to jump up and down about because it's still way off in the ocean and it could very well peter out before it comes anywhere near land. Most of them do.

But they're watching it, just in case.

Meanwhile, it might pass over a scattered island here or there, and those folks are getting wet.

Your Content Marketing Tropical Disturbance

In the course of building your Content Marketing Hurricane, you'll hit "tropical disturbance" stage when you're ready to actually take action yourself and it culminates in creating and distributing your first several pieces of high-quality content.

But the actual production of content is surrounded by a cycle of events that needs to constantly spin like the winds in that storm. Here they are:

1. **Initial decision making** – figuring out which of the intersecting points is going to be your topic(s) of choice to build your content around.
2. **Finding a niche** – fitting that topic(s) into a marketable niche with an established or identifiable target audience and (possibly) competition.
3. **Narrowing the focus** – positioning yourself within that niche in such a way that you can successfully market to a broad enough audience while handling the competition.
4. **Deciding on the media** – choosing the channels and formats most effective for the content you want to produce and audience you need to speak to.
5. **Creating your content** – (we'll discuss this in far more detail in Section Three: Tropical Depression!)
6. **Getting published** – distributing that content effectively on your own or via one or more 3rd parties.
7. **Re-evaluating** – monitoring and analyzing the entire process with an eye for efficiency and efficacy; seeing what worked and repeating it, seeing what didn't work

and eliminating it.

In Section Two, we'll take a deeper look at each of these steps and we'll determine the best way to use each to constantly build the momentum of your Content Marketing Hurricane!

11 WHAT DOES IT TAKE TO CREATE A TROPICAL DISTURBANCE?

As you'll see clearly over the next few pages, a closely related question is:

What does it take to create an *expert*?

Because that's really one of the key goals behind an effective content marketing strategy, especially for beginners who are just getting involved in content marketing to help them reach their personal or business goals: they need to establish themselves as a go-to source of valuable information in their chosen field – an expert that others respect and turn to for guidance.

So that's an interesting question, isn't it?

What does it take to create an expert?

Of course, you know what an expert is, at least on the surface. But, what really makes someone an expert?

When you get right down to it, it's *perception*. Someone *appears* to be an expert, and so we look to them *as* an expert.

Did you catch that?

In other words, being an expert doesn't mean that person is smarter, or works harder, or knows the right people, or anything else (although those things can probably help.)

It just means that person *appears* to be an expert. And so, the natural human reaction is to treat them that way.

The Oprah Principle

Do you want a perfect example of this principle at work?

Turn on reruns of Oprah, or any other daytime talk show for that matter. Turn on The Today Show, Good Morning America or Jason and Kelly.

At some point on nearly every episode of this type of program, the host will start discussing an interesting topic, and will soon introduce an author who has "just written the book on..." whatever the topic is.

Now, when that man or woman walks out on stage, with a beautiful spinning graphic of their new book highlighted in the corner of the screen and their name lit up across the bottom, what do you think about that person?

You automatically assume they are an expert on... whatever the topic is.

After all, they've "written the book" on it, haven't they? What other proof do you need?

And they haven't even opened their mouth yet.

Now, for the next three minutes, or however long the segment lasts, assuming you're interested in their topic, you're going to hang on every word coming out of their mouth.

You'll quote bits and pieces to your friends later in the day. You'll save an "I told you so" for your spouse later that evening, because an expert just agreed with you. You'll quite possibly head out and purchase that book for yourself, if your interest is piqued enough, or at least remember the title when you're at the library the next time.

As far as you're concerned, this individual knows what he's talking about. Not because his view is so well-thought out and logical, or because he's supported it with iron-clad evidence, necessarily.

But simply because *he said so*.

And he's an expert.

You need to be published

If you're interested in joining the ranks of the experts you see on the talk shows every day, you're going to have to get your thoughts out to the masses in a way they automatically respect.

You're going to have to get published.

After all, there's really only one guaranteed difference between the author being interviewed by Oprah and the potentially millions of other people watching the show who may know more than that person does about the subject Oprah's discussing with him.

That difference is, he wrote the book!

If YOU wrote the book, Oprah would be talking to YOU, not him.

So, for just a moment, let me help you over a mental barrier.

Your mental barrier to being an expert

You see, becoming an expert in a field in which you're knowledgeable may sound overwhelming to you.

There may even be some voice in the back of your mind telling you things like,

"You're no expert."

"You're a fake."

"No one cares about this topic."

"No one is ever going to read what you write."

"You don't even know how to write."

"There are a million people who know more than you do about this topic."

"You're wasting your time."

It is vital that you understand one thing before moving forward with the process contained in this section:

Anyone can do this

Absolutely anyone can become a renowned expert in the field

of their choice if they are willing and able to follow the process outlined in these pages.

There are no barriers to entry based on age, race, social status, finances, geography, intelligence or aptitude. There are no evil forces conspiring to keep you from creating your Content Marketing Tropical Disturbance. There are no current experts in the field of your choice who are going to be threatened by your entry onto the scene.

The only possible barrier to your becoming an expert in the field of your choice is YOU.

So, if you're ready to focus on what I've dubbed **The Instant Expert Formula**, and you're willing to put the time and effort into following the formula consistently, you're already well on your way to building your Content Marketing Hurricane!

12 THE INSTANT EXPERT FORMULA

In this chapter, you'll get a quick overview of The Instant Expert Formula, a guide to boosting your reputation by putting your thoughts in concrete form and getting them published.

As noted in the previous chapter, the basis of the formula is earning expert status by harnessing positive public opinion through the almost magical power of publication.

You should have also noted the fact that anyone can accomplish this with the right level of desire, motivation, and hard work. (Especially if you're working with subject matter you truly have a passion for.)

By combining those qualities with the information contained in this section, YOU can quickly start taking advantage of the benefits that come from being an expert!

This is not a scheme

It's important to note that the Instant Expert Formula is NOT a get-rich-quick scheme. I'm not promising you oodles of cash just by following a set-it-and-forget-it process.

As a matter of fact, I'm not promising anything... except this:

If you're truly passionate about your subject, you're willing to put the time and energy into working the formula and constantly improving your content creation and marketing skills, you WILL see results.

I can't tell you exactly what those results will be, but I can tell you that you will be satisfied if you work this system well. And if things don't work out as you wish, you can always go back and tweak the system to improve.

Are you ready?

The Instant Expert Formula

As noted in the introduction, the Formula, in a nutshell is:

1. Initial decision making
2. Finding a niche
3. Narrowing the focus
4. Deciding on the media
5. Creating the content
6. Getting published
7. Re-evaluating

The Formula can also be expressed in the form of a flowchart, because, as we'll discuss, it's an ongoing process, much like the spinning of your storm.

The Instant Expert Formula

As you can see, the process is simple. The technology is readily available

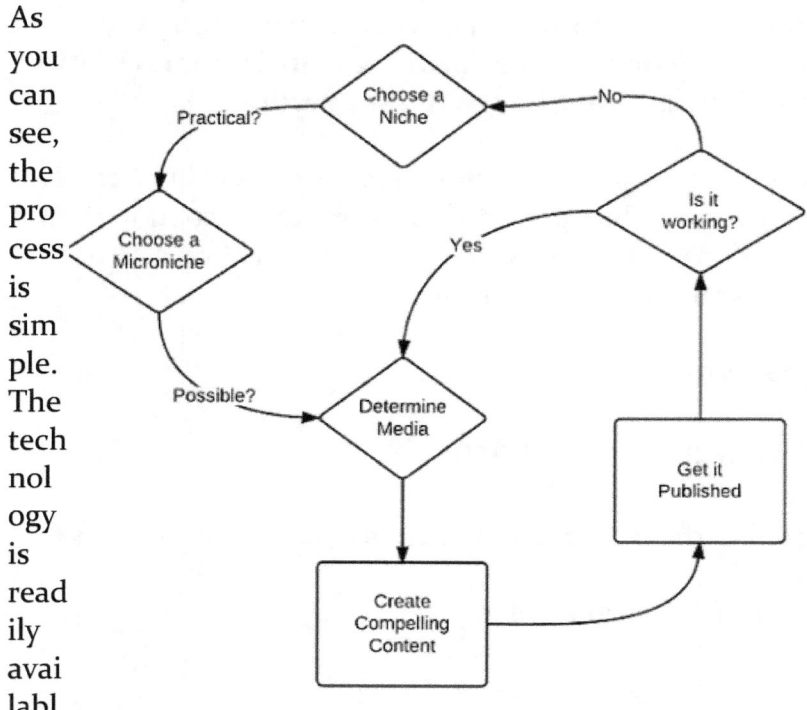

e to nearly everyone. When that technology is combined with the ease with which you can research, evaluate and add to the body of knowledge on a niche topic, the potential becomes truly incredible.

The next seven chapters will delve deeper into each of the seven steps in The Instant Expert Formula, helping you take action quickly and easily so you can truly experience the "instant" aspect of this powerful process!

But for a moment, let's look at a snapshot of each step:

1. **Initial Decision-Making**: Here is where you will take the topics you've brainstormed based on your unique

"disparate forces" and hone them to truly capitalize on expert status. The exercises you perform in this chapter will help you focus your efforts on the best possible topic(s) for YOU.

2. **Finding a Niche**: Once you have a topic in mind, this chapter will help you narrow that topic down to a reasonable niche by helping you carve away the aspects of that topic that are either not of interest to you, not of interest to your potential audience, or both.

3. **Narrowing the Focus**: This time, the focus is tightened even more as you transition your topic from a niche to a micro-niche, clearly identifying your target audience and coming away with a crystal-clear idea of what you will need to do to position yourself as the authority on that particular area of study.

4. **Deciding on the Media**: Now that your concept and your target audience are clearly defined, you can begin to explore HOW you are going to reach your audience with your information. The potential outlets for your knowledge are nearly endless, so you'll have to weigh the pros and cons of each to come up with the perfect recipe for micro-niche domination.

5. **Creating Your Content**: Here's where the tires really hit the road. Since you know your topic, your audience and your target media options so well, you're ready to actually translate your thoughts into publishable form. Although I'll touch on them here, in Section Three I'll give you a ton of solid tips and tricks to make sure nothing gets lost in that translation.

6. **Getting Published**: Once you get your thoughts out on paper or screen, this chapter will help you make sure it goes somewhere other than your personal hard drive. We'll discuss various methods for publishing your material, both traditionally and non-traditionally.

7. **Re-evaluating**: After going through the entire process

you are in an excellent position to look back and see how things went. The beauty of a formula like this is that you can go back and make adjustments constantly to improve your performance and/or add to what you've already created. This chapter will help you do just that.

Remember, what I'm providing is simply a guide. I can't answer the questions I'm presenting for you. And if you want to get the most benefit out of this information, you're going to want to answer them honestly yourself.

As you work your way through this section, you should be able to clearly watch your own unique "disparate forces" coalescing into a powerful "tropical disturbance" that is quickly building power and momentum.

So, without any further delay, let's get into Chapter 13, Initial Decision-Making.

13 INITIAL DECISION MAKING

The first step in the process of moving from just a bunch of "disparate forces" to actually creating a "tropical disturbance" is to ask some in-depth probing questions to unmask which of the intersecting points you've identified has the legs to carry your storm all the way to land and beyond.

In other words, which topic(s) are you both *interested* in building as an expertise, and *capable* of doing so?

To begin the process of becoming an expert, you're going to need to spend some time quietly contemplating the answers to some very important questions.

Don't rush this process. Give it the time and attention it deserves.

The answers to these basic questions form the foundation of the entire formula. Therefore, if you rush through, do a shoddy job answering these questions, or allow yourself to get caught up in trying to force the answers you "want", you're only hurting yourself and your chances of success.

So schedule at least an hour or two away from the job, the family and the Boob Tube to sit in a quiet place with a pen and notebook in hand.

The following list of questions is designed to help you focus your thoughts. They should be answered in the order presented because the questions are designed to naturally narrow your focus, with each one building on the one before.

Not every question will end up being vital to your final outcome, but many will. So, to get the most power out of this process, don't skip any.

Keep an open mind

As you're going through the questions, it's important to keep an open mind and turn off your internal editor.

We all know what he sounds like:

"Come on, that's ridiculous. You'll never be able to do that."

"Who are you kidding? You don't know anything about that."

"Ha! You? An expert? Give me a break!"

The fact is, this nasty little guy can stop you in your tracks and kill your motivation to reach your goals before you even have those goals established.

So make a conscious effort right now not to let him do it.

As you're reading and responding to these questions, especially in the beginning stages, make sure you're answering honestly and realistically, but at the same time, creatively and optimistically!

These aren't commitments. Not yet. These are possibilities,

and they're wide open for the time being.

So, while you want to be "realistic", don't let reality hold you back from considering some great ideas.

Don't automatically assume that your passion for organic hot pepper farming is completely outside the realm of what you're looking for here.

The fact is, if you have a passion for – and knowledge about – a particular subject, and you just love learning and talking about it, (unless you're really, really weird,) other people may feel the same way!

So answer these questions as broadly as possible for now. We'll worry about prioritizing and weeding out the weaker ideas later.

For now, have fun with it.

Questions to ponder:

So, if you completed Exercise #9, you reviewed those intersections where the forces that made you who you are come together, and you should have a short list in front of you of topics or ideas that truly fire your imagination and make you want to talk.

Although it may be difficult, you're going to need to look at that list objectively for a few minutes and ask yourself the following questions:

- What on that list do you care enough about to discuss in depth for perhaps the next several years?
- What on the list do you have a hard time not talking

about?
- Why do you care so much? (This one's very important. It digs to the core of your motivation. If you're not sure, or if it's a rotten motive, it might not stick.)
- What subject(s) on the list do you already know like the back of your hand?
- What on the list do friends, family, and coworkers already ask you for advice about?
- Would any of them want to pay you for that knowledge? (Again, this is key. For some of you, you're eventually going to want to sell your knowledge. But even if that's not your content marketing goal, the content you create needs to be valuable enough that your audience would pay for it if it wasn't free.)

Asking these questions and answering them objectively lays a beautiful foundation on which you can build powerful content.

It separates those areas you love for reasons that will last from subjects you may tire of quickly. It separates topics you may love but which are not marketable from gems that people would be willing to pay for. And, it offers the opportunity to determine what niche your Content Marketing Hurricane is going to draw the most "moisture" from.

That's what we'll get into next.

Exercise #10 – Brainstorming: Deciding on Topics
1. On a new piece of paper, or in a new document, answer each of the questions posed on the previous page, in order.
2. Remember: honesty and an open mind are key here to be sure you're identifying all the realistic options available.

3. Read the next chapter.

14 FINDING A NICHE

If you're keeping up with the program, you should now have a seriously short list of topics that absolutely float your boat, and that you would be more than happy to talk about for years to come with anyone who's willing to listen. And, chances are very high they'll be willing to pay you to do just that.

So, why, at this point, do we need to find a niche? Isn't a handful of awesome topics good enough?

No, not really, and here's why:

A quick word on targeting

As you continue to develop your content marketing strategy, you're going to be targeting a specific audience of people who you need to speak to.

Many brands make the mistake of trying to "target" pretty much anyone with a pulse and a wallet.

But that's not targeting. That's even less effective than not targeting at all, because at least when you don't think about targeting your content will tend to seek out people like you.

But truly effective content needs to be exclusive to those folks who are truly intended to benefit from it, and that can't be everyone.

Here's how Tom Fishburne of Marketoon Studios explained this[6]:

> "Your target market is not the same as anyone who could conceivably buy your product. A target market is deliberately exclusive. That niche focus is what gives your message teeth. It is what compels consumers to identify with your brand. It is what gives you insight to speak to them so clearly."

A niche is a frame

By identifying an established niche (or, if you're very brave, inventing one) you are able to more easily identify who makes up your target audience. You're also able to easily identify who is already marketing with content to that audience and how they're doing it.

Both of these revelations are absolutely vital to the success of your strategy, and must be determined early so that knowledge can guide you as you continue plotting your course toward land. Your niche is the frame in which you can clearly see that picture.

So, to determine which niche you will attack, ask yourself

---

6   "Why Your Content Marketing Riches Can be Found in the Niches", Content Marketing Institute, (http://contentmarketinginstitute.com/2013/03/content-marketing-riches-niches/)

these questions:

- Can the topic(s) you have chosen be broken down to be more specific? (For instance, rather than choosing "fly fishing", could you choose "fly fishing for brown trout" and still feel as passionate about the subject matter?)
- If so, are any or all of the subtopics complementary? (In the above example, if you could start by marketing around the topic of "fly fishing for brown trout" and it turned out successful, couldn't you easily parlay that success into a discussion of "fly fishing for steelhead"?)
- Does the name of an already-established expert in the field come to mind?
- Are you prepared to compete with that person for the attention of the target audience?
- If so, how are you different? (This is another key question that reaches the heart of marketing: how we convince a prospect we/our product/our service is different and therefore better than another.)

Just as was the case with the last set of questions, this set may weed out an idea or two you had fallen in love with. Don't worry about that! You would have figured it out eventually anyway. By deciding to drop it now, you save yourself time and money down the road.

And at this point, you probably only have one or two topics left standing.

But don't worry, we're going to shave it down just a little bit further next.

Exercise #11 – Brainstorming: Finding a Niche

1. Using the results of Exercise #10, answer each of the questions found on the preceding page.
2. Google is your friend here: spend some time researching your topics to identify subtopics you may not have considered, and to identify experts in those fields.
3. Don't self-edit when identifying how you're different. We'll get to that. For now, list every way you can think of.
4. Read the next chapter.

15 NARROWING THE FOCUS

Now that you've settled on one or two niches that fit well with your preferences, your passions, and your abilities, we need to narrow that focus even more. Hopefully all the way down to a microniche: the true secret to a powerful Content Marketing Hurricane!

A simple example: Local Search

To give you a simple example of how narrowing your focus will lead to a more powerful content marketing strategy, consider the example of Distinctive Landscaping.

As reported by Hubspot[7] the company's president, Jason Scott, recognized that his competitors were not taking advantage of online search. Many of them didn't even have a website.

Now, at this point, Distinctive Landscaping could have put up a site and started loading it up with tons of fantastic content about lawn care, planting and trimming, fertilizing, and a host of other topics of interest to their target audience: people who needed their property cared for.

---

7   "Case Studies: Distinctive Landscaping", HubSpot Inbound Marketing
     Blog, (http://www.hubspot.com/customers/distinctive-landscaping)

But there was a very important narrowing of the focus that was required first.

You see, like most small businesses that offer physical services (such as landscapers, construction firms, cleaning companies, etc.) Distinctive Landscaping has a limited geographic area that they service. They're located in North Attleboro, Massachusetts.

What would have been the use of Distinctive Landscaping becoming known as landscaping experts all across the internet if 99.9% of their traffic was coming from Alaska or Singapore?

What they needed was to become known as landscaping experts in the towns surrounding North Attleboro, Massachusetts, where their actual target audience resided!

In comparison to the broad subject of "landscaping", there are a number niche topics they could have chosen. But instead of focusing on "pruning your perennials", what made the most sense for their unique target audience was to focus on "landscaping in and around North Attleboro".

And at this point, they're the undisputed go-to source, dominating search results for towns in that vicinity.

That's the power of narrowing the focus as you're creating your content marketing strategy.

The fish and the pond

Remember the old adage, "he's a big fish in a little pond"? Well the idea of identifying a microniche can be explained by picturing that fish and that pond.

For example, if your subject is Marketing, you're diving into a virtual ocean of information. There's room in that ocean for thousands of world-renown experts, many of which will never even meet each other.

But, if you were to narrow that subject down to the subtopic of Social Media Marketing, you're starting to get somewhere. Now you're in a large lake, but at least you can see the land nearby.

To narrow the field even farther, you could decide to limit your expertise to Mastering Facebook for Business.

Now that's a niche. You're swimming in a narrow channel where the water is calm and there's only room for a few folks to really enjoy themselves.

If there's enough water there, you may even be able to settle on a microniche. In our example above, that might be something like Helping Self-help Authors Master Facebook to Boost Book Sales and Build a Platform.

Whew! That's a serious microniche! If you can narrow your topic down that far, you're standing in a very deep puddle, with room for just one world-renown expert, and you've got some serious profit-building and reputation-boosting potential in your hands!

As long as your microniche will still provide you with a large number of interested audience members, you're still passionate enough about it to make it a prime focus of your life, and you can still have fun with it...

Your Content Marketing Hurricane is going to dramatically speed up with the laser-focused guidance of that microniche!

Combining microniches

Can you combine more than one microniche?

I'm glad you asked that.

You certainly can, and most content marketers who have narrowed their focus do market to more than one microniche at a time. However, it's important to realize that, to be truly effective, each microniche has to be treated as its own project that will only tangentially connect to other complementary microniches.

For example, the marketer who makes a success of the microniche used in our example above could very well use many of the same principles (and therefore, content) to help authors of other kinds of non-fiction books master Facebook, but the target audience will be very different.

So, although the individual may know more than enough to make a success of that microniche as well, it's not going to be automatic. It's going to require a reworking of the strategy and massaging of the content to make it applicable to the new audience, and therefore have a chance at the same level of success.

So, work on one microniche at a time and don't sacrifice quality for convenience if and when you decide to expand into new areas.

Exercise #12 – Brainstorming: Narrowing the Focus

1. Using the results of Exercise #11, determine how narrowly your niche topic(s) can be sliced while still maintaining a viable audience, and keeping your interest.
2. Read the next chapter.

16 DECIDING ON THE MEDIA

As your "tropical disturbance" continues to build momentum, you're drawing closer to that all-important first piece of content.

But, you've probably already noticed that a successful Content Marketing Hurricane requires a lot of planning and preparation. Otherwise, it'll just fizzle out over the open sea and no one will ever know it existed.

So the next step you'll need to consider as you prepare for that first creative effort is the huge range of media options available to you as a budding content creator.

We'll go over specific examples with a lot more information in Section Three, but for right now, let's just take a bird's eye view of what's available:

Written Content

The majority of the content being created is in written form. And this makes sense, since it translates easily to the various channels through which content is delivered and consumed, as well as all the devices we use to consume it.

It's also the medium that most content creators are most

comfortable with because it doesn't require that they stand up in front of a crowd or a camera. It doesn't even require their voice. It just requires their mind, limited typing skill, and access to a computer.

Creating written content is one of those skills – like playing some musical instruments – that's easy to learn but difficult to master.

It's fairly quick and easy to throw something together and get it in front of people if you have a mediocre grasp of the language and an internet connection. But to really shine with written content requires time, patience, and practice. Not to mention an appreciation for the masters that have come before.

Of course, as you look through this list and consider your own topic(s) and your own preferences, you may find that written content is not your first choice, so keep an open mind as you review this list of potential written content:

- Blogs
- Articles written for online article banks
- Press Releases
- Social Media updates
- White Papers
- e-Books
- Newspaper articles/columns
- Newsletter or e-Newsletter articles/columns
- Trade magazine articles/columns
- Consumer magazine articles/columns
- Autoresponders
- Brochures
- Pamphlets
- Books

Drilling down into written content

Yes, written content is relatively easy to produce and distribute.

But that doesn't necessarily mean it's the very best option for your specific Content Marketing Hurricane. And that's important to realize.

Written content is probably the first thing that comes to your mind when you consider creating something, but you'll need to ask yourself whether your target audience would really prefer an article over, say, a video or a podcast.

You'll also want to consider whether your writing ability (or your aptitude if you still have some practice ahead of you) can make written content shine, or if you would achieve greater success with a different medium?

After you get a grasp of written and verbal content – as well as how the two can be combined – you'll be in a better position to make your selections and test them out.

But for right now, let's assume you have an acceptable grasp of the language, and your target audience is happy to consume written content. Here are some details for you to consider:

Blogs and Online Articles

I consider a blog to be one of the most powerful means of marketing with content – especially at the beginning – because of a few factors:

- **Cheap** – You can start a blog and keep it going indefinitely for free. Or, for a whopping $3 for a domain name and $60 for a year of hosting, you can establish a permanent web presence.
- **Fast** – It literally takes a few minutes to set up a blog on any of the major platforms. If you know your subject matter well, you can knock off a solid blog post in an hour or less, and with the right automation at your fingertips, distribution takes seconds.
- **Flexible** – While the bulk of your blog content will likely be text-based (hence it's appearance in this category), blog posts can include images, audio, video, presentations, and any number of rich media combinations as well. The major blogging platforms are intentionally created very flexible with plugins and addons in order to promote creativity and personalization.
- **Powerful** – From a content marketing standpoint, a well-written blog post combined with the most basic SEO knowledge is about the most effective means of attracting attention on search engines that exists. Google loves blogs because they provide fresh content regularly. If you take some time to think about the terms your audience uses to search for information about your topic, you can easily craft titles and blog post content that fulfills their needs and will show up when they're searching.

Still need some convincing? Check out these blogging stats as reported by IgniteSpot.com[8]:

- Small businesses with blogs generate

---

8 "The Blogconomy Infographic", IgniteSpot, (http://ignitespot.com/small-business-marketing-idea/)

126% more leads than businesses without blogs.

- **81%** of U.S. consumers trust advice and information from blogs.
- Companies that blog enjoy **97%** more inbound links.
- **61%** of U.S. consumers have made a purchase based directly on a blog post.
- **70%** of consumers learn about a company through articles rather than ads.

Can you tell I'm a fan of blogging? It's my number one weapon of choice for my own content marketing efforts, and it's done wonders for my own Content Marketing Hurricane.

Not to detract from other forms of online articles, but all of the above applies to articles created for reputable online article banks as well.

(Although, when you get right down to it, you're going to have a better chance of building your own Content Marketing Hurricane around a property you own – like your own branded blog – than around a mass of articles scattered across the web.)

Social Media

Personally, I tend to use social media primarily as a distribution tool for other content I create and as a means of locating people and companies that I'd like to be connected to.

I also share a lot of interesting things I find online that I think will be of benefit to my audience of followers.

But a lot of content marketers successfully take this a step further by actually creating bite-size content specifically for the social networks they are active on. Google+ seems to really be a magnet for this style of content marketing and I've come across a number of very talented marketers who are going to town on G+.

One of the key benefits of creating content specifically for social media is that it can become a powerful vehicle for engagement – generating conversations and building relationships – with your target audience.

Unlike posting articles or distributing e-books, content created specifically for social media channels tends to spark real conversation. Years back, a blog could accomplish this via the comments section, but these days, unfortunately, blog comments are primarily a place for self-serving marketers to sneak in a backlink to their own websites, and rarely evolves into real engagement.

For an eye-opening glimpse into the power of social media take a look at these stats, pulled together by Digital Insights[9] and current as of the publication of this book:

- There are over **1 billion** unique monthly visitors on YouTube.
- Social Media generates almost **double** the marketing leads of trade show, telemarketing, direct mail, or pay-per-click advertising.
- Instagram photos get over **1000** comments per second.
- Over **1 billion** endorsements have been

9 "Social Media Stats 2013 Infographic", Digital Insights (http://ignitespot.com/small-business-marketing-idea/)

`shared on LinkedIn`

- The Google+ +1 button is appears online more than **5 billion** times per day.
- Over **400 million** tweets are sent each day.
- Facebook has over 1.15 billion users worldwide, and over **90%** of them check their accounts at least once daily.

Newspapers, Newsletters and e-Newsletters

While the local daily newspaper is slowly going the way of the dodo, it's not dead yet. And from a business standpoint, it still can impress some pretty important people, especially if your target audience is local.

Writing articles for the local newspaper, or penning a regular column, still proves to be a very effective content marketing strategy for professionals like doctors, lawyers, and accountants. It also works well for authors who are marketing their books, and business leaders looking to expand their local expert status.

Smaller newsletters can also work well if they're popular with your target audience.

As a special note, e-Newsletters, used as a means of staying in touch regularly with e-mail subscribers on a home-grown e-mail list is probably second on my list after blogging as a powerful and flexible force in building your Hurricane.

The real secret to the power of newspapers and newsletters is the habitual nature of their readership.

Unlike blogs, most of which are read sporadically and only

succeed in securing a limited percentage of their readership as subscribers, nearly 100% of a newspaper's readership gets the paper on a daily or weekly basis. And, if they're paying for that subscription, there's a very good chance they habitually set aside a portion of their day or week to sit down and peruse the paper.

If you're featured regularly as a contributor to that publication, you're going to become a familiar presence in that person's life. And before they even actually know you, they begin to like and trust you.

And that is content marketing gold.

Trade and Consumer Magazines

Just like newspapers, print magazines may be dying off, but they're not dead yet. And you'd have a hard time finding another mass media with a more targeted audience on the hook than a trade magazine that's established in a particular industry.

Most established trade magazines have digital versions available already, and at some point in the future, they may all switch over to digital-only. That doesn't change their value.

Trade magazines provide a fantastic opportunity for content marketers because – in the case of the most popular examples – subscribing to them is almost a right of passage for decision makers in that industry. For that reason, you can be sure that if your article appears in that trade magazine, a huge percentage of your target audience is going to read it.

Consumer magazines tend to have a broader appeal, but

there's still a demographic and psychographic majority that each consumer mag appeals to. If your target audience includes many members of that demographic, you're going to grab a lot of eyeballs with a well-written article in Cosmopolitan or Us.

Pamphlets, Brochures and Books

The physical "thud" effect of a book still can't be beat for establishing your status as an expert in your field. Smaller printed works like brochures and pamphlets can also be quite impressive under the right circumstances.

For instance, as part of a direct mail package to a targeted list of prospects, a book or brochure printed professionally with your name on the cover has to turn some heads.

As another special note, e-Books are becoming absolutely huge! They're not just cheap .pdf downloads selling for ridiculous prices online. They are now a perfectly legitimate and recognized form of publishing that is within everyone's reach.

Writing a quality e-Book and publishing it via the Kindle format gets you on Amazon.com as a published author, which can be worth the effort in and of itself. (Special Hint: Amazon can be a fantastic source of testimonials and referrals as well, thanks to their powerful review and suggestions features!)

There are plenty of other options for written content available, but you get the point. So keep your eyes open as you consume content yourself, and make note of other options that come across your radar and may work for your own Content Marketing Hurricane.

Verbal Content

The options available are less varied with what I've labeled as "verbal content", but don't take that to mean it's less powerful.

As a matter of fact, in many ways spoken content can be a more powerful force in your Content Marketing Hurricane because it captures attention more readily, does an even better job of branding you as an expert in your field, and offers you priceless face time in front of your targeted audience that a blog post or a white paper simply cannot accomplish.

The big downside, of course, is that you have to get up in front of people and speak about your topic, and that's nearly impossible for some due to overwhelming stage fright.

But, if you're capable of doing so with skill and dignity, you can capitalize on that by getting involved in:

- Seminars
- Workshops
- Speeches
- Recordings (of all of the above, or original)

Drilling down into verbal content

As noted above, verbal content can be even more effective than written content for accomplishing some content marketing goals.

Why?

- **It's more visceral** – By leveraging the full impact of body language, facial expression, vocal inflections AND your words, you have a far greater opportunity to reach your audience's heart AND their mind. This is both more effective initially, and more memorable in the long run.
- **It's the better option for visual lessons** – If you're explaining something like how to build a birdhouse, you can get all the information out there in an article, and you can even include some quality illustrations to make it a little clearer. But you'll never be able to teach your reader as well in an article as you can by letting them watch you build a birdhouse step-by-step. It simply translates better visually.
- **Some people are visual learners** – For some people, even if the subject matter could be easily and effectively put across in writing, they're just going to appreciate it and benefit from it more if they're seeing or hearing it rather than reading it.

Speeches

Simple speeches at the local Chamber of Commerce breakfast or the Rotary Club, or keynote addresses in front of thousands... regardless of the size and format, if you're willing and able to get up in front of an audience and talk about your subject of choice, you're going to garner attention.

A short speech can be quick and easy to prepare, and yet be powerful in its effect.

As an added benefit, most opportunities to speak in front of a crowd are automatic networking opportunities as well. As a speaker on the program, you'll naturally attract the attention of those audience members, providing a perfect ice breaker for conversations before and after the speech.

Seminars and Workshops

A seminar can be as simple as a series of speeches that follow an educational course outline. In many cases, these are not only powerful in their effect on your content marketing efforts, but are also a source of revenue if managed properly.

The benefit of a seminar over one or more speeches really depends on the content you're trying to get across and how involved in the learning process your audience needs to be. If some extensive back-and-forth questions and answers would be beneficial for them, a seminar setting may be best. If a lot of hands-on experiential learning is more appropriate, a workshop may work better.

As you develop your content marketing strategy, you'll need to determine what level of time, energy and money you can dedicate toward this channel. If allowed, it can become all-consuming, especially if you're handling all the event planning yourself.

But, if running seminars and workshops proves to be the most effective content marketing weapon in your arsenal, it can be, not only effective from a marketing standpoint, but very lucrative as well.

Recordings

For true Content Marketing Hurricane benefit, making an audio and/or video recording of any speech, seminar, or workshop you deliver makes all the sense in the world.

This allows you to multiply the value of each occurrence, extend its reach beyond the limited number of attendees, and use that content permanently for repurposing and even the addition of revenue streams as your strategy progresses.

Although you may have your personal preferences between verbal and written content, you'll likely find – as most content marketers do – that a combination of the two types works best to attract and convert the most members of your target audience.

Combining the Two

Another increasingly popular form of content creation made feasible by the online craze encapsulated in YouTube, iTunes, and Slideshare, requires combining writing skill with a willingness and ability to put yourself out there in front of the audience, at least to an extent.

- Online video
- Podcasting
- Slide presentations

Video

With YouTube holding its place as the second most popular search engine online, and the increasing popularity and efficacy of mobile video, adding online video to your Content Marketing Hurricane should be high on your priority list.

Even if you shied away from the public speaking route because of stage fright, you can likely make a success of starring in your own online videos through detailed planning, script writing, and practice.

Since you don't actually have to *see* your audience looking at you, and you have the luxury of going back and re-recording any part you're not happy with, there's a way to fit video into your comfort zone.

Of course, you don't have to star in every video you make. There are plenty of other options including videos made from screen captures, PowerPoint presentation slides, combined still images... the options are nearly endless.

But, since one of the main benefits of video is the way it draws your audience to the human side of what you are discussing, don't eliminate yourself (or at least some human being) from the equation completely.

To get a handle on just how powerful online video has become from a marketing standpoint, take a look at these ten statistics curated by Strothers Communications Group on their 41 Stories blog[10]:

- About **46%** of people say they'd be more likely to seek out information about a product or service after seeing it in an online video.(Source: Eloqua)
- Video is now the sixth most popular content marketing tactic, as **70%** of B2B marketers use some form of online video with their overall strategies.(Source: Eloqua)
- Of the **80%** of internet users who watched a video ad, **46%** took some sort of action after viewing the ad.(Source:

---

10 "Top 10 Stats Behind the Power of Video Marketing", 41 Stories, Strother Communications Group, (http://www.scgpr.com/41-stories/the-power-of-video-marketing)

Video Brewery)

- The average user spends **88%** more time on a website with video. (Source: Mist Media)
- Video and e-mail marketing can increase click-through rates by more than **90%**.(Source: Mist Media)
- Video equals higher viewer retention. The information retained in one minute of online video is equal to about **1.8 million** written words.(Source: Brainshark)
- Video attracts two to three times as many monthly visitors, doubles their time spent on the site and has a **157%** increase in organic traffic from search engines. (Source: MarketingSherpa)
- Blog posts incorporating video attract **three times** as many inbound links as blog posts without video.(Source: SEOmoz)
- **59%** of senior executives prefer video over text. (Source: Brainshark)
- Having video on the landing page of your site makes it **53%** more likely to show up on page 1 of Google.(Source: Mist Media)

Podcasting

While technically some podcasts employ video, for the sake of our discussion, we'll consider podcasting to be the audio side of the equation.

Podcasting has proven to be a quiet explosion of content for years now. The premise is simple: anyone can record themselves speaking, upload it to iTunes and a number of other podcasting services for free, and have their recordings streamed to subscribers automatically to be perused at their leisure via their iPods, in their car, on their morning run, or wherever.

Using this basic formula, many content marketers have built huge audiences of avid listeners who tune in for every episode, engage with the podcaster via comments and links that accompany the recording, and become rabid brand evangelists as a result.

If you can get used to the sound of your own voice, and are interested in exploring the creative options available in podcasting, you can consider it an audio blog as it has basically the same potential.

Presentations

What used to be the boring "necessary evil" of the board room is now the darling of the content marketer: slide presentations.

Thanks primarily to SlideShare, especially after its acquisition by LinkedIn, slide presentations created on PowerPoint or a number of other popular applications can be easily distributed across the internet.

These presentations often employ stunning visuals, emotive backing music or narration, and sparse but powerful text to tell stories that each of those media by themselves could not.

But the key to the effective use of presentations – as it is with videos and podcasts – is a strategically written script.

The script doesn't need to be anything formal, but it's important that the backbone of the script exist before the video, podcast, or presentation is created. Otherwise, it's very easy for one of these media to fly off track and lose its value to your Content Marketing Hurricane.

This has been a lot to take in...

As we'll discuss in more detail going forward, each of the different media and the channels available to distribute them have their own pros and cons, and no content marketing strategy is required to use all of them.

But every content marketer should *be aware* of all of them, and stay on top of new avenues and technologies for content creation, distribution, and consumption as they appear.

The key, as always, is to pick and choose strategically what is going to work best for you and your target audience, and always keep adapting as needed to keep your Content Marketing Hurricane spinning.

Exercise #13 – Brainstorming: Deciding on Media
1. Using the niches and microniches you identified in the previous two exercises, choose which forms of media make the most sense for the target audience you're going after.
2. Remember to take into consideration your own abilities, likes and dislikes as well. But, don't rule something out that you can learn to be comfortable with.
3. Read the next chapter.

17 CREATING YOUR CONTENT

We've done a lot of preliminary work: pulling together your unique "disparate forces", determining where they intersect and which topics you're going to have the best chance of successfully using to market with content, then prioritizing and narrowing the focus based on your own preferences, your strengths and weaknesses, and the market itself.

Now, finally, after all this effort, you're ready to sit down and develop that very first piece of stellar content that's going to go out into the world with your name on it.

Are you ready? This is exciting!

We're going to spend a lot more time breaking down content creation in Section Three where your Content Marketing Hurricane reaches "tropical depression" stage. At that point, you're going to be focused on continually creating and distributing content based on the cycle we've been discussing.

Just as that evolving storm out over the ocean begins to spin around a central eye once the conditions are right and it begins drawing power from the wind and the water, your Content Marketing Hurricane needs to "spin" too.

That is, you need to have some established systems in place

that allow you to create and distribute content efficiently and effectively or else the work is going to overwhelm you and you'll end up just churning it out to get it done.

And that won't accomplish anything for you.

But to get this cycle moving in the right direction, your mind needs to be in the right place.

So let me introduce you to **The Four Laws of Effective Content Creation**. Then, later on, we'll get into the nitty gritty of actually creating all the various kinds of content you can use to build your strategy.

Law #1: Focus

The first law has to do with keeping your subject reasonable narrow.

Thou shalt limit thy main points.

Each time you prepare to write a piece of content, you'll need to plan it out in such a way that it is narrowed down to a set number of well-defined main points.

Then, as you build off that outline, be sure to express your thoughts on these points clearly and concisely. Don't add any unnecessary filler or try to impress someone with your wordiness.

Based on the media you choose, this focus may bring you down to just ONE main point. That's OK. Cover that point well.

Law #2: Express Yourself Clearly

While maintaining a narrow set of points is important, those points do need to be covered well.

Thou shalt cover thy main points effectively.

Research your points well and always check your facts. Nothing will slow down your momentum like losing credibility with your audience. It's definitely not worth it for expedience.

Then, express your information as clearly and concisely as you can while still helping your audience. Simple points and simple thoughts can still be helpful as long as you're not talking down to your audience or dumbing down the subject unnecessarily.

But, at the same time, don't shortchange your audience by only giving them the surface facts if both you and they know there's a lot more there under the surface.

Dig deep and give it to them!

Law #3: Be Yourself

The third law speaks to those points of differentiation you identified earlier.

Thou shalt develop thine own voice.

While you're obviously going to be utilizing the work of content creators that went before you, don't try to emulate their voice. And by no means should you EVER plagiarize another person's content in any way.

Instead, assimilate the information, run it through your own filters, and express it with your own unique flavor.

This is a powerful form of differentiation that will eventually form one of the key success factors in your content marketing strategy.

Law #4: Have Fun

It may seem strange to create a law that obligates you to have fun, but that's because too many content marketers forget this vital piece of the puzzle.

Thou shalt have a blast.

If you're not having fun, it will quickly shine through in the crappy content you create. So don't do that to your audience or to yourself.

This is a lot of work, but it's also fun, exciting, and – in the long run – profitable!

So have fun with it!

Exercise #14 – Creating Your First Piece of Content

1. Now it's time to create that all-important first piece of stellar content. Based on the decisions you made in Exercise #13, choose one type of media and one channel that makes sense for you and your target audience.

2. For now, don't be overly concerned about making this one piece perfect. Instead, focus on following The Four Laws of Effective Content Creation and getting over the "I don't know what I'm doing" hump.
3. When you're done, do the Happy Dance.
4. Read the next chapter.

18 GETTING PUBLISHED

Realizing we're going to spend a lot more time on content creation in Section Three, we're going to move right along now to the next step in the Instant Expert Formula cycle.

While creating stellar content is key to a successful Content Marketing Hurricane, distributing that content effectively is just as important. Just as closet writers have known for centuries, you'll never sell a novel that stays in your desk drawer.

For the sake of discussion, I'll divide the myriad options for content distribution into two major categories: traditional publishing and self-publishing.

Traditional Publishing

While the dusty old machine we call "publishing" still exists, and certainly provides a viable outlet for distributing your content in the form of books to a wide audience, there's a lot more to the traditional publishing distribution channels.

Traditional publishing involves anyone other than you distributing content on your behalf.

The big publishing houses in New York can do that for you,

and if you're lucky enough to pick up a publishing contract, they can make a lot of things happen very quickly for you.

In fact, if you're able to secure a publishing contract for your book, or you're able to have one or more of your articles published – either online or offline – by a large recognized media establishment, it can do wonders for your Content Marketing Hurricane!

However, let's keep it real: the lines are long and your chances are slim. So slim, in fact, I wouldn't count on it at all. That way, when it happens, it will be a pleasant surprise.

What does traditional publishing offer?

The publishing industry is and always has been a marketing machine. The actual printing of books or magazines is really secondary to the marketing of ideas and (on the magazine side) the sale of advertising.

So, when you plug into that machine, you can potentially see your visibility skyrocket very quickly. Publishers know how to generate buzz around a book they're backing, and magazines have their finger directly on the pulse of their audience, so they know how to present your article in the most favorable light.

Of course, you need to understand that no book publisher is going to handle *all* the marketing for you. It's expected that an author will push his own work as vigorously as possible, and in fact most publishers won't consider gambling on a book if the author doesn't already show some aptitude for doing so.

But working in conjunction with a publisher or a large

magazine is going to make the job of obtaining visibility and capitalizing on it far easier and quicker than a self-publishing content marketer can hope to expect.

In addition, traditional publishers can offer priceless editorial support and expertise. Often, especially if you're immersed in your subject for a long time, creating content piece after content piece, you can become immune to your own faux pas. An experienced editor can keep your idiosyncrasies in line with a brief phone call, opening your eyes to errors you've been making, perhaps for years.

What are the cons of traditional publishing?

When you publish your content through a traditional industry media, you often relinquish most if not all control over that content.

This essentially eliminates the possibility of repurposing that content in other ways, limiting to some extent the value of the original time and effort expended.

In addition, since every book distributed by a traditional publisher is a financial gamble, they're going to be quick to pull the plug on the entire arrangement just as soon as it becomes apparent it's not going to be a best seller.

So, should your book not sell as well as they'd like, you may find yourself high and dry before you get anywhere.

Having articles published through magazines will rarely put you in that position, but you may find an approved assignment being 'killed" unexpectedly prior to publication, even at the last minute, meaning any time and effort you've put into promoting that article's publication will have been for nothing.

Of course, in that case, you can generally still use the article you wrote in other ways, even offering it to another magazine.

So the bottom line is not to discount or ignore traditional publishing just because it's not the flavor du jour. But, at the same time, don't spend your last dollar and last drop of sweat struggling to get published traditionally because other effective options do exist.

Self-publishing

Years ago, self-publishing was a way to quickly spend a ton of money on nothing more than a little ego stroking. The term "self-published" was synonymous with "not good enough to be really published."

Fair or not, that was the image self-publishing conjured up in peoples' minds. They saw a struggling author tired of rejection stacking dozens of boxes of books in his garage that will never see the light of day, and proudly displaying one on his coffee table for guests to drool over.

The traditional publishing community thumbed their noses at self-published authors, book stores and libraries refused to carry their books, and most readers were not open-minded enough to look past all that and try out a book that looked and sounded unprofessional.

But these days, self-publishing is not only easy and cheap – even free – it's also gained a lot more respect in the content marketing world than it ever had in comparison to traditional publishing in the past.

From a content marketing standpoint, self-publishing refers

to any form of content distribution that you are able to control yourself.

A lot of the content distribution channels we've already touched on fall under this category, and all of them are viable options for content marketers with content their target audience wants to consume.

Again, here are some options:

- P.O.D. (print on demand) book
- White paper or brochure (for offline distribution)
- Direct mail
- Physical newsletter
- White paper (for online distribution)
- E-mail newsletter
- Podcast
- YouTube video
- Blog article

The Modern Self-publisher

Today, self-publishing has taken off in numerous forms, primarily due to two technological advances in publishing that synergistically strengthen each other: P.O.D. publishing, and the Internet.

Whereas a self-publisher in 1988 could easily spend tens of thousands of dollars to see his book into print, and was then wholly responsible for marketing and selling the hundreds of copies he was forced to purchase for the smallest print run, getting a book published in trade paperback today costs nothing up front, costs a few dollars for the printing and shipping of *one copy* and can be completed in an hour or so.

Then, even more incredibly, not another copy needs be printed *unless it sells*! That's the true beauty of print-on-demand publishing services like CreateSpace, LuLu, and others.

Combined with the cost savings and convenience of P.O.D. technology is the ease with which these books can now be marketed and sold via the Internet.

If you publish your book via CreateSpace, for instance, it becomes automatically available on Amazon.com, the single largest book seller in the world. And even if you don't use CreateSpace, getting your book on Amazon only takes a few minutes.

Hundreds of other online retail sales sources are available as well for free or close to it, not to mention the ability to sell directly from your own website with nothing more than a free PayPal account and a few minutes of coding.

Social networking, e-mail marketing, blogging, and being active in niche communities online all allow a self-published author to build a platform, build credibility and buzz, and end up selling a self-published book faster and more effectively than even a traditionally published book that makes it to Barnes and Noble's or Borders, and with a higher profit margin to top it off.

When you also add in the increasingly viable option of e-book publishing (such as via the Amazon Kindle format) the profit margin and scalability increases even more.

So are there any cons to self-publishing?

Honestly, not much.

The only real caveat that must be understood about self-publishing – whether you're talking about a full-length book, a white paper, or even a simple blog post – is that marketing your content and getting it into the hands of your target audience is completely and totally up to you.

No one is going to do that work for you, at least not at the start. There is no gigantic marketing machine behind your content, like there is for a James Patterson or a Stephen King. There is no team of publicists covering all the bases to make sure absolutely everyone knows that you've just self-published your e-book.

That's all up to you.

So, if you're up for it, self-publishing is a low-cost, high-yield opportunity to add tremendous power to your Content Marketing Hurricane!

In conclusion...

There are pros and cons to both categories of content distribution.

The most obvious pros that come to mind are speed, ease, and low cost on the side of self-publishing (with the exception of physical newsletters and direct mail which will incur printing and mailing costs), and access to potentially huge unearned audiences in the case of traditional publishing.

On the other side of the coin, traditional publishing is unpredictable and subjective. You and, to some extent, your content, are at the mercy of The Editor or whomever is in charge of the publication in question. They can pull the plug, require untold edits, and basically make your life difficult if they want to.

Self-publishing requires a lot of work on your part, and also requires that you identify and reach your target audience on your own, which generally means a slower rise to success and a longer learning curve.

But, in both cases, stellar content that is strategically distributed to reach the target audience it was best suited to appeal to will likely succeed.

Exercise #15 – Publishing Your First Piece of Content
1. Polish up that piece of content you created in Exercise #14 as best you can (we'll discuss that more in the next section) to get it ready for publication.
2. Self-publish your content using one or more of the options outlined in this chapter. Again, don't worry too much at the moment about how perfect it is or even how strategic it is. This is just to get past the "I've never done this before" stage.
3. Reach around and pat yourself on the back.
4. Read the next chapter.

19 RE-EVALUATING

As I noted at the beginning of this section, once your storm reaches the "tropical disturbance" stage, it starts spinning around a central eye as it continues to build strength from the wind and water around it.

Aptly illustrated by that spinning storm, your effective content marketing strategy creates a continuous cycle in which re-evaluating the effectiveness of every piece of content you create provides the necessary final step that allows you to restart the cycle with renewed confidence and skill.

Monitoring Your Content

As each piece of content is distributed, your predetermined strategy should have dictated what you expect that piece of content to accomplish.

In some cases, the goal could be very simple, such as gaining a certain number of visitors or a certain level of engagement on social media channels. Or, for other content pieces, you may be moving a visitor along the sales funnel toward an eventual sale or repeat sale.

In all cases you need to be sure you can monitor the effectiveness of that piece of content so you can determine how successful it is and use that precious knowledge to inform future content creation and distribution choices.

Monitoring online content

One of the most common monitoring tools available today for online content is Google Analytics.

Although it can be somewhat intimidating to begin with, a lot of really great tutorial information exists online and Google itself provides very detailed help features along with this comprehensive, free analytics tool. A number of other paid and free options exist as well, some of which work along with Google Analytics, others of which are fully independent.

In an excellent blog post on the subject of what metrics content marketers need to be most interested in, Convince and Convert's Jay Baer[11] had these recommendations:

> Content cannot be measured with a single metric, because no one data point can successfully or satisfactorily tell you whether your program is working. Instead, you need to create an array of metrics that are selected from four primary buckets:
> 1. Consumption Metrics – answering the question "How many people consumed your content, measured as page views, downloads, or views?"
> 2. Sharing Metrics – answering the question "How often do consumers

---

[11] "The 4 Types of Content Metrics That Matter", Jay Baer, Convince and Convert, (http://www.convinceandconvert.com/content-marketing-2/the-4-types-of-content-metrics-that-matter/)

    of your content share it with
    others?"
3. Lead Generation Metrics – answering
   the question, "How often do content
   consumers turn into leads?"
4. Sales Metrics – answering the
   question, "How often do content
   consumers turn into customers?"

By covering all these bases, you'll be in an excellent position to determine how effective each piece of online content is from a business perspective.

Of course, your own personal and business goals play a large part in determining which aspects of this monitoring effort matter most to you.

For instance, during the initial deployment of a content marketing strategy, it makes sense to focus almost exclusively on the level of consumption and sharing occurring with your content.

However, a year into the strategy, if your content is being consumed and shared like crazy, but isn't generating any sort of leads or sales, it's failing, pure and simple.

Monitoring offline content

For offline content, monitoring its effect is a trickier job.

Direct response advertising principles can apply to much of the content you produce offline, assuming your goals for the content include some sort of engagement with the audience.

For example, including a direct response device, such as a coupon or order form, along with a call to action asking readers to turn the device in can give you some solid numbers to work with as to the effectiveness of your content.

Likewise, using offline content to push people toward your website via mobile QR code, or coupon codes can help bring offline interactions and advertising into the online analytics realm, making it easier to track.

A real old-school, but still effective, method of tracking the effectiveness of offline content in real world situations is to ask customers, "how did you hear about us?" or any other question that's appropriate to your situation and gives you insight into what promotional tools are working, and which ones may need some fine tuning.

If the content is strictly informational, such as a book, then sales figures may be your only offline option for monitoring its success, but you can be creative with this and eek more information out of offline sales than meets the eye.

For example, many authors have been very successful at creating large audiences online by including additional, unpublished information on their website that is made available for free – but only to people who have purchased their book.

From a monitoring standpoint, any time you can move transactions online, you have a much deeper and richer wealth of information at your fingertips.

Using That Information

The second half of the re-evaluation equation is using the information you gather to constantly improve your content marketing strategy.

I like to think of this aspect of content marketing as a form of *kaizen*, a principle responsible for the incredible technological and industrial turnaround that occurred in Japan after WWII.

The basic concept involves continuous improvement through tiny, incremental, logical changes to what you're doing and how you're doing it.

Toyota is famous for requiring any line worker who notices and abnormality in an automobile part or process during assembly to stop the entire line and immediately involve a supervisor in order to initiate "a kaizen event": discussing potential improvements to the part or process in order to improve the entire product.

And we all know how dominant Toyota has been for decades now in global automobile sales, so the concept works.

Six Sigma® and other similar quality control processes are based on a similar idea. You can apply the same philosophy to your content marketing strategy.

As you're constantly monitoring your outgoing content and how it performs, you may notice, for instance, that your videos are enjoying a slightly higher level of engagement than your text blog posts.

That doesn't mean you automatically scrap your blogging and put all your efforts into video content. It means you incrementally test variations in the current strategy to help optimize your blog content to take advantage of what appears to be an audience preference for video. And you keep monitoring and making those adjustments until your total strategy success rate improves.

Likewise, if you put out two display ads in two local papers, one with the headline, "Eat at Joe's!" and the other with the headline, "Kids Eat Free at Joe's!" you should be able to determine fairly quickly if your target audience cares about bringing their kids in for a free meal. If they don't, then you know that that particular promotion probably isn't a winner for your audience. You move on to something else.

This is a huge subject, and this book isn't the place to truly give it the treatment it deserves. We will discuss some more aspects of monitoring as we get more into targeting and other related subjects in the next two sections.

But for now, we'll leave it that continuously monitoring your content efficacy and using that information to apply constant incremental improvements to your strategy is the single best way to get that Content Marketing Hurricane spinning faster, and heading toward land!

Exercise #16 – Monitoring Your First Piece of Content

1. Based on the publishing method used in Exercise #15, review your options for monitoring that content.
2. Set a reminder to check back on the content's progress in a day, a week, and a month.
3. Don't worry if no one ever sees your first piece of content. The beauty of self-publishing it online as that it will live forever and you can always go back and use it again later. But if you do notice you've sparked some interest, make note of what sorts of reactions you get and what kinds of people you attracted.
4. Use the insights you gain from this monitoring process to determine how to improve your content for the next time.

5. Read the next chapter.

Section Three: Tropical Depression

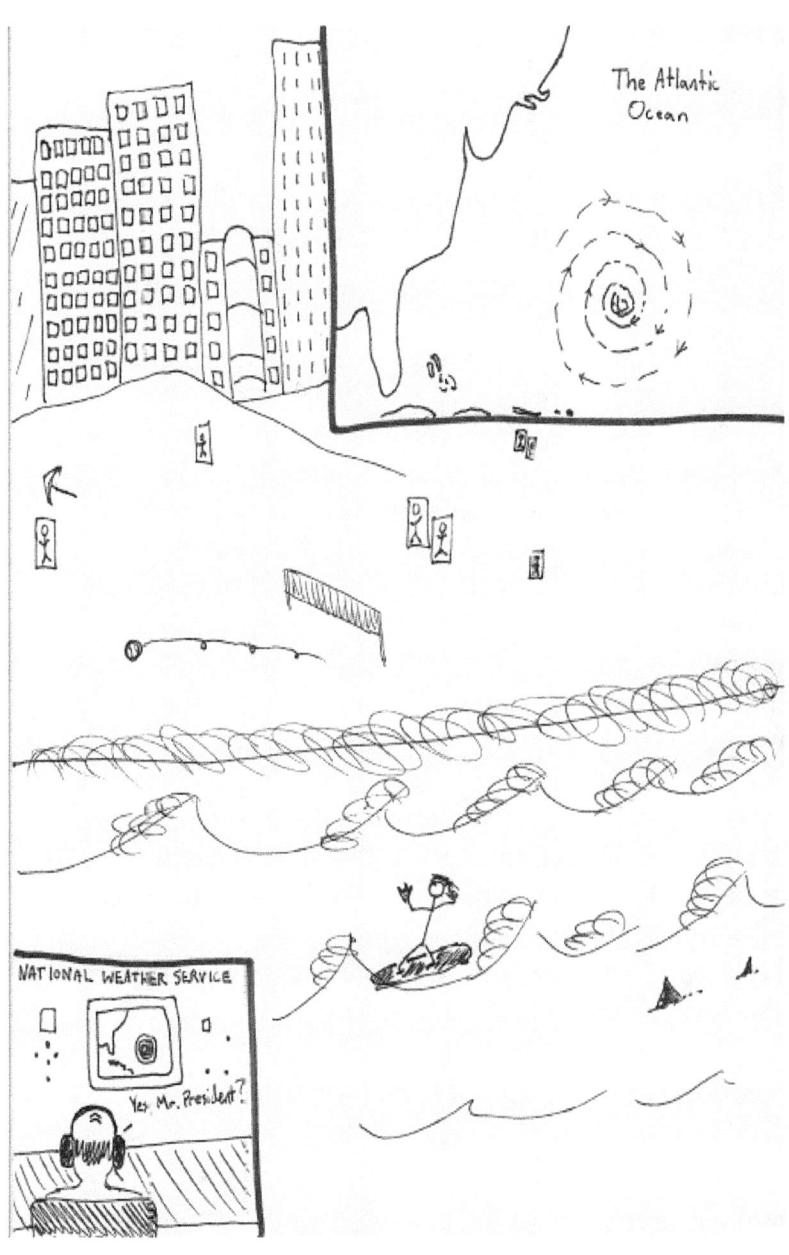

20 WHAT IS A TROPICAL DEPRESSION?

If you've made it this far, you've come a long way.

Your ideas have been narrowed and honed to laser precision. You have a solid picture of your target audience, your competition, and your own positioning in the market. You've also planned out, created, and distributed that all-important first piece of content. And you're monitoring its success as you go along.

At this point, the Instant Expert Formula cycle – the spinning of the storm – is in full swing.

So, now is the perfect time to really dig down deep into creating stellar content and making those incremental improvements (kaizen) we discussed in the last chapter.

In our Hurricane analogy, you're now heading into the third stage of storm growth: Tropical Depression.

What does the Tropical Depression stage involve?

As you continue to create your content, you're going to want it to constantly build off what's already been created and increase in strength, reach, and effect.

That doesn't mean, of course, that every single piece of content is a sequel to the last, or that you're simply cutting a larger content piece into bite-size pieces and laying them out one at a time like a trail of breadcrumbs. (Although that kind of idea does work under certain circumstances, and should be included in your strategy if you want to experiment with it.)

Rather, it means that none of your content exists in a vacuum. Every piece you create, regardless of the format, the media, or the purpose, will be informed by, and possibly even refer to, what has come before it.

Depending on the purpose, it may make sense to directly call out points you've made previously when distributing a new piece. (For example, internal links in one blog post that bring a reader back to a previous post that provides additional topical information.)

And, at the very least, even if it's not communicated to your audience, *you* know what's gone before, and you can use that knowledge to your advantage.

That's why, during the "tropical depression" stage, you're not only getting the attention of the meteorologists watching your storm's progression, but now those folks that live on the coast are starting to keep an eye on you too. They can tell you're gaining strength and you're headed their way. Maybe you'll get to them, maybe you won't.

But you can bet they're paying attention.

We're going to discuss the following ten steps in the "tropical depression" content creation process:

1. **Think About Your Audience** – Targeting your content to solve a problem for your audience.
2. **Plan Ahead** – Creating efficiencies and guaranteeing success.
3. **Get Excited** – Putting your personal best into every piece.
4. **Write Like You Speak** – Making your content conversational and engaging.
5. **Limit or Eliminate Jargon** – Avoid one of the biggest problems rookie content marketers make.
6. **Trust Your First Draft** – It came out this way for a reason, so trust that.
7. **Proofread** – Get the technical junk out of the way.
8. **Read Aloud** – Verify the content is conversational.
9. **Trash Your First Draft** – Get it right the second time.
10. **Know When to Let it Go** – Concentrate on excellence, not perfection.

As you become more proficient at creating content, these steps will become second nature, and you certainly won't need to check them off like a to do list. But, to start with, that's how you should consider it:

A 10-Step Checklist for Creating Killer Content!

21 THINK ABOUT YOUR AUDIENCE

No matter how many pieces of content you've created, or how good you think you are at doing so, I would advise you to always take the time to think about your target audience before creating another piece.

You see, it's very easy to slowly but surely stop talking to your audience and start talking to yourself. After all, you're the person you know best, and therefore, you're the easiest person to speak to.

And creating content for yourself is going to do about as much good as talking to yourself would.

In an effort to assist American small business owners to improve their communications, the National Criminal Justice Reference Department of the Federal Government put together a "Communications Toolkit" that listed "Know exactly who your audience is and look at everything from that group's point of view" as Principle #1 in their list of social marketing principles.[12]

There honestly aren't many areas in which I can truthfully say

---

[12] "Think Like a Marketer – Know Your Audience", NCJRS, (https://www.ncjrs.gov/ccdo/toolkit/marketing/know.html)

I agree with the government, but this is one of them:

It is crucial that you understand who your target audience is and then look at the world from their point of view. You have to have an intimate understanding of the people you are trying to reach in order to motivate them to take action.

This just makes sense from a content marketing standpoint.

If you don't have a solid picture in your mind of who your target audience is, you're not likely to speak to them in any meaningful way as you create and distribute your content.

Don't waste your time.

Instead, before you sit down to write or flip on the camera, ask yourself these questions:

What do they already know?

This question speaks to the knowledge level your target audience is already at when they begin to consume the content you're creating.

It will help you determine how much background explanation may be necessary, how deep you can delve into the topic at hand, and what sort of terminology you can and can't freely use.

It also helps you to get a feel for what they *expect* from your content.

With this information at your fingertips, you can begin to determine where the gaps are in your audience's understanding, and fill those gaps with your content.

What do they care about?

There may be plenty that they don't already know about the topic you want to discuss. But if they really don't care to learn about it, you have two choices: you can either discuss some truly compelling reasons why they *should* care, or you can scrap the idea and choose something that your audience will actually want to consume.

Without taking this into consideration, you run the risk of alienating your audience, and eventually losing them completely.

In content marketing, hatred is not the opposite of love.

Boredom is.

What pain points do they suffer?

This is sales terminology, but it applies equally well to content marketing.

Generally, people are going to be interested in relieving their pain – whether physical or metaphorical. If you can determine what makes your audience angry, frustrated, scared, stressed out, miserable, exhausted, guilty, envious, insecure or confused, then you know what's going to interest them.

The next logical step is to create content that will in some way relieve that pain, whether you're offering a legitimate solution to a problem, a better understanding of the problem and how it affects them, or just a means of forgetting about it for a few minutes.

An important caveat, though: Don't assume you know your audience's pain. Do the research, ask the questions, learn from them. Few things will piss someone off quicker than being left behind while you jump to conclusions.

What questions do they have?

Directly related to the audience's pain points is the list of questions they likely have about your product, service, or topic.

In many cases, these questions will seem elementary and silly to you, but that's because you're immersed in your topic day in and day out. To the casual reader, something that's second nature to you could be a revelation.

If you have access to customer service representatives that work with your target audience, you have a prime source for content topics because they're being asked questions all day every day.

But even if you're on your own, just thinking logically about your topic from the viewpoint of someone with little or no knowledge should help you generate a long list of legitimate questions one or more members of your target audience likely has rolling around in their mind.

What do you want them to do when they're done?

This helps you to consider where your content will reside along the conversion funnel you've set up as part of your overarching business strategy.

One of the dumbest and most costly mistakes content marketers make is to finish a fantastic piece of content and send it out into the world without including a clear call to action.

Believe me, no matter how beautifully written or produced, and no matter how clever or insightful your content is, if your audience doesn't know what to do with it, they'll do absolutely nothing.

Is the piece purely informational? Then perhaps the only goal is to interest them enough to click through to a different article or to learn more about you as a content provider.

Is this a lead generation piece? Then you're going to need to include a call-to-action that will result in your obtaining their contact information.

Is this a sales letter? Then ultimately, a converted sale is the goal and your content needs to reflect that so the audience knows what you want them to do next.

Targeting 101

The very best archer in the world is going to miss 100% of the time if he can't see the target.

That seems embarrassingly simple, but it's true.

If you're going to "hit" your target audience, you have to see them very clearly so you can accurately line up your shot.

So, let's discuss some details regarding identifying and targeting your audience:

Demographics

One way to target specific groups or individuals within those groups is by means of demographics.

Demographics refer to grouping people by age, sex, nationality, level of education, where they live, where they work, etc.

The use of demographic information to make general decisions about people might rub some the wrong way. It's not politically correct.

But from a marketing standpoint, it's just common sense.

Upper middle class white males aged 55-65 living in Florida are likely interested in different products and services than poor Asian females aged 12-15 living in Vietnam.

From a content marketing standpoint, the same potential differences apply to what information the target demographic(s) would be interested in consuming, how promotional messages should be approached, and how likely successful conversion is.

Of course, collecting demographic information is an inherently touchy situation.

You can always include basic demographic information as part of any sign-up form you include on your website. But, the more you ask for, the less people are going to fill out your form, so this could be self-defeatist.

Privacy laws and common decency prevent you from demanding demographic information from anyone, so marketers need to be creative in how they obtain the limited demographics at their disposal.

The most common and effective method involves offering free content in exchange for information, such as a white paper in exchange for contact information. Once you have an individual s e-mail address, you can introduce additional non-prying surveys to the e-mail mix to gain further demographic details from your list.

Of course, this method requires that you make some educated guesses as to what initial content will appeal to your target audience in order to write that first white paper.

You may very well need to experiment with topics and offers until you find your target audience coming to you, then begin building your strategy more completely around them.

Psychographics

Now psychographics are a little tougher to pin down in concrete terms, but they're ironically easier to learn from the way people interact with your content.

They're not qualities you can see on the outside, or on a balance sheet. They have to do with how we *think*.

Personality, attitude, values, interests and lifestyle are all areas covered by psychographic segmentation, and they're definitely a tricky thing to work with.

But, just as is the case with demographics, while individuals will fall outside the bell curve, psychographic generalizations can be incredibly accurate and valuable for the majority.

While a group's psychographic profile may not preclude an entire product or service as cleanly as broader demographic data can, it will have an even greater impact on how you craft your messages, how you tell your story, and how slowly (or not so slowly) you introduce your offer.

The Adzerk blog offered a fantastic example that shows how demographics and psychographics differ from a marketing perspective and how psychographics can help focus your targeting efforts more effectively[13]:

> As an example, consider athletic shoes - from a demographic point of view, a broad range of people are in the market for the product, from young to old, both men and women, for all kinds of reasons. From a psychographic perspective though, some customers might care most about performance, while others concern themselves with the fashion appeal of the product, while still others just want a particular brand as a status symbol. For a shoe company to maximize sales, it needs to understand these trends to design the right products, and talk about them the right way.
>
> You need only look at major shoe retailers to see the model in action - endorsements from celebrity athletes for the performance crowd, options to customize the colors and materials for the fashion crowd, and rare, limited editions for the status conscious crowd.

---

13   "Audience Targeting 101: Psychographics", Adzerk blog, (http://adzerk.com/blog/2012/05/audience-targeting-101-psychographics)

From an advertising perspective, the
brand talks to one crowd very different
than another, so the ads on ESPN are
very different than on SneakerNews.com.
There's no doubt that shoe companies
fully understand the demographic
qualities of each customer base, but in
many ways, the psychographic elements
are what really drive the products,
positioning, and sales.

Interestingly, demographics and psychographics work
exceptionally well together because people in the same age
group and/or living in the same area tend to develop similar
attitudes about certain subjects, have shared the same
cultural milestones, and are likely to view your content
through a similar lens.

Of course, the last thing you want to do is make any
unfounded assumptions about your audience based on some
convergence of demographic and psychographic data.

These days, technology has bridged gaps that used to gape
wide open between generations, genders, social and economic
groups.

Give your audience the benefit of the doubt and let them tell
you if you're wrong.

Customer Personas

Combining demographic and psychographic information
allows you to create a living, breathing, 3D image of your
target audience (metaphorically speaking, of course.)

In the marketing world, this is called a customer persona (or buyer persona), and a well-crafted example is the Holy Grail of marketing departments everywhere.

Tony Zambito, the marketer who originally coined the phrase "buyer personas" explained their importance to content marketing in a recent article on his blog[14]:

> Although the buyer persona story consists of a few sentences, it breaks down the complex to a level of meaningful simplicity, which can often be missing in content creation. And, this is what we want. To enable sharpened focus on what we need to understand about buyers at a particular stage. Buyer Persona Stories offers a powerful technique for teams to get on the same page about buyers.

By developing customer personas that match the major groups that make up your target audience, you can create your content with a personal, conversational voice that speaks directly to that one person's heart.

Although you and I know you'll be distributing this content to potentially thousands of people, each one that consumes that piece of content (and that falls into the persona you crafted it for) will feel like it was made *just for them*.

Exercise #17 – Identifying Your Target Audience
1. Recover your notes from Exercises #10-16 and review

---

14 "Accelerate Content Marketing Effectiveness with the Power of Buyer Persona Stories", Tony Zambito, (http://tonyzambito.com/accelerate-content-marketing-effectiveness-power-buyer-persona-stories/)

them briefly.

2. All those exercises touched on your target audience to some extent. Based on what you learned in this chapter, make any adjustments you'd like to what you wrote previously.

3. Now consider your first piece of content and any ideas you have for future pieces. What can you do right now to better identify the demographic and psychographic characteristics of the target audience you want those content pieces to appeal to?

4. Create one or more customer personas for your target audience by combining what you know about them and what you can comfortably imagine. Then do some Google research to test your assumptions and polish the persona.

5. Read the next chapter.

22 PLAN AHEAD

I can almost hear you now: "Plan ahead? It seems like we've been planning ahead for over 130 pages already!"

And you're right, we have. I'm glad you're sensing that pattern at this point.

But there's still a little more planning needed here.

Remember, at this point, we're not planning your strategy, or any other macro element of what you're trying to accomplish. This is part of the content creation process.

We're planning ahead for the *next content piece*.

Before you start hammering out a headline and lead paragraph, before you start scripting that killer video intro, you need to take some time to plan it out.

Ask yourself these important questions:

What is the position in the buying cycle/sales funnel?

Never divorce your marketing messages from the sales or buying cycle you're working with.

While many people have jumped on the content marketing bandwagon when it comes to lead generation – feeding leads into the top of the funnel through search optimized content – there are dozens of content marketing tactics that work exceptionally well for all other points in the funnel too.

In an excellent article created by LEBSEO Design[15], the correlation between content and the different stages of the buying cycle was explained this way:

1. **Interest/Awareness** – At this stage of the cycle, you're aiming to earn permission to pitch yourself later on. *Content Format Ideas*: Blog posts, memes, entertaining video, guides, whitepapers, podcasts.
2. **Consideration / Establishing Preference** – In the consideration stage, customers have identified a need and are actively seeking out potential solutions. *Content Format Ideas*: Targeted landing pages (with competitor comparisons), spec sheets, demo videos, tutorials, case studies, "about us" page/brand stories, testimonials, reviews, whitepapers, eBooks, informational events.
3. **Purchase / Decision** – Having evaluated their options, the lead is ready to make a purchase decision. *Content Format Ideas:* Spec sheets, competitor analysis, demonstrations and tutorials, ROI calculators, direct response e-

---

15 "Mapping Content to the Buying Cycle", LEBSEO Design Blog, (http://www.lebseodesign.com/2013/09/mapping-content-buying-cycle/)

```
mails and landing pages, pricing
information, reviews & testimonials,
coupons and special offers.
```

4. **Evaluation and Repurchase** – Your audience began as strangers, but at this stage they've become paying customers. The goal from here is to turn those customers into loyal customers and advocates. *Content Format Ideas*: Feedback forms and surveys, special offers, promotional deals, newsletters, blog posts, members-only events.

By effectively mapping your next piece of content to the stage of the buying cycle you're hoping to cover, you can make your content creation faster and easier by narrowing your choices, and you can be sure to approach the piece in the right way.

What information does the audience need to move forward?

See, you're leading the audience somewhere. You need to be a good guide and feed them the information they need to get where you want them to go.

If that's heading toward a sale, then there's a lot of information they're going to need. You'll need to establish credibility, explain all the reasons why your product or service is the best, and why it's worth the price you're asking, then you'll need to ask for the sale.

If the content you're creating is just intended as a small step (for instance, an educational piece intended to establish credibility) then the information requirement isn't as high.

Always include every bit of information your audience needs to accomplish your purpose, and not a word more.

Why should they care what you say?

As with all advertising or marketing messages, you absolutely must take a step back from your own zeal and look at what you're creating from the customer's perspective.

Generally speaking, the average audience member approaches every one of the thousands of messages that comes at them throughout every day with the same basic attitude: "so what?"

If you don't have a really good, well thought out answer to that question that you can provide within the first 3-5 seconds they're previewing your content, you've lost them.

Here's how Alyson Cravens of eCoast Sales[16] explains it:

```
What's in it for me? The content you
create will speak to your potential
prospects by answering that single
question. If your content is egocentric,
few people will be interested in
learning more about your services, your
brand or anything you want to promote.
```

Losing an otherwise qualified prospect over something so fixable... that's just wrong.

What is the logical next step?

---

16 "The Value of Great Content Marketing", Alyson Craven, The eCoast Blog, (http://blog2.ecoastsales.com/2013/11/22/the-value-of-great-content-marketing/)

As noted above, you're leading your audience somewhere. So what is it you want them to do next?

This is where you develop your call to action. And how important is a call to action?

Pratik Kanada at The App Entrepreneur[17] explained it this way:

> Once on your page, and after reading through your content, visitors are looking for somewhere to go next. Many a times, the website visitors leave the site only because they do not know the next step; there is lack of a clear call to action. They may be looking for more information, or maybe to subscribe to your newsletter or maybe even make a purchase! There are a number of possibilities and call to action buttons give the users a direction in which to proceed, a variety of options that they can pick from.

If you don't include a direct request for the audience to do something, they're going to consume your content, then move right along to the next message zooming toward their eyeballs and you'll be forgotten within seconds.

So while you have them, make sure you tell them what to do next.

---

17 "Call to Action – How Important is It?" Pratik Kanada, The App Entrepreneur blog, (http://theappentrepreneur.com/call-to-action)

Exercise #18 – Planning Ahead for the Next Content Piece

1. Review your customer persona(s) from Exercise #17, and the overarching conversion funnel you've already created.
2. Answer the four questions from this chapter with your next content piece in mind.
3. Read the next chapter.

23 GET EXCITED

It may sound strange to list "get excited" as one of the steps to creating killer copy and building your Content Marketing Hurricane, but think about it:

You've read enough in your life to know the difference between lively and dead copy. When a writer's not excited about what he's going to write, it comes through crystal-clear in the words he manages to wring out of his bored mind.

They lie there on the paper, not moving, their life force gone.

And after a while, they really start to stink.

Remember, back in Chapter 8, we discussed Your Passion as being one of the important Disparate Forces that helps build your Content Marketing Hurricane. You've done exercises to help narrow down your subject matter to something you're passionate enough about to maintain excitement over the long haul.

There's an important reason for that.

Without being able to honestly get excited and interested each and every time you sit down to create a piece of content, your entire storm is going to lose momentum.

So get excited about what you're about to create. Think about the positive effects of communicating this information effectively to your audience:

- Are they going to gain benefits from consuming your content?
- Will they become more knowledgeable?
- Wealthier?
- Healthier?
- Happier?
- Or, will *you* benefit from sending out a spectacular blog post or white paper?
- What new prospects will you locate?
- What new sales will you generate?

Then get excited!

This is exciting stuff!

Exercise #19 – Get Excited
1. Get excited*
2. Read the next chapter.
*Yes, seriously. If you're not excited, how can you expect your audience to be? Liquor is optional.

24 WRITE LIKE YOU SPEAK

Now it's time to get into the actual nitty-gritty of creating great content.

I'm going to be developing this section as simply and straightforwardly as I can because, frankly, there's way too much potential information for me to realistically stuff into this book.

To maintain continuity, I'll be discussing content creation from the standpoint of writing something because, with very few exceptions, some sort of scripting or outline is necessary even for non-written content.

Understand, however, that the basic principles discussed in the next few chapters apply equally well to creating videos, audio recordings, podcasts, and (with minor variations) visual content as well.

The first thing to consider is the manner in which you write your content. Your tone, and your unique voice.

"Write like you speak" is an age-old mantra among direct mail copywriters, but it translates equally well into nearly every other form of writing outside of some fiction.

It seems like a really simple tip to put into practice, but it's not always as easy as it seems.

Why do you do it?

From a very young age, we are taught that when we write words down, they have to be perfect. Every grammar rule must be perfectly measured, every T crossed and every I dotted. We scored extra points for longer words, and got to learn very quickly how to write fancy enough to impress our English teachers.

The problem is, with very few exceptions, our intended reader is not our English teacher!

So living, breathing copy that really reaches the heart of our audience is going to sound far more like an informal conversation than a textbook essay. Even if the purpose is strictly informational, and the subject is potentially dry, if we write it the way we would discuss it sitting on the couch in our friend's living room, we'll make the words come alive for our reader.

How do you do it?

The easiest way to accomplish this (at least until it becomes second nature) is to make some brief notes about the points you want to cover in your content piece, perhaps in an outline form, then move away from the paper or keyboard and just review the outline.

Imagine you've been asked to speak to a small group about this subject and these are your notes.

Or, if that intimidates you, imagine your best friend asked you a question and these are the points that are going to make up your reply.

Then, simply talk it out.

Once you've spent a few minutes forming your verbal argument, you'll start to get a sense of the kinds of words and transitional phrases you're naturally using to make the points understandable and to keep the "conversation" flowing.

If you can anticipate questions that your audience may naturally have as you speak, all the better: these give you an opportunity to add clarifying information without overwhelming the piece by trying to stuff too much into it.

And if some humor weaves its way into the content because that's your natural personality, so much the better. Few things draw an audience to you like a natural, funny voice.

When you've contemplated your verbal version of the content for a few minutes, return to the keyboard or paper and try to duplicate, as best you can, the exact words and phrasing you were using when you spoke.

It will probably be a little rough around the edges when you first get it all down on paper, but the rough draft you have to work with at that point will be far closer to your ideal final draft than the 10th grade English essay you were going to write.

A caveat:

Now, this tip does need to be taken with a grain of salt.

For instance, if you tend to have a foul mouth, or a racy sense of humor, you'll need to rein them in for the sake of decency and professionalism.

If the subject matter you're discussing is particularly charged, controversial, or in some other way requires a higher level of decorum than your normal speaking manner may convey, you'll want to keep that in mind as you draft and complete your content piece. (Remember, it's still the audience and the goal of the content that finally determines its format and tone, this is just a guideline.)

But, as you've probably noticed throughout this book, a liberal sprinkling of conjunctions (you've, we'll, etc.) makes the text far easier to read because it sounds less formal.

You may have also noticed that the text isn't dumbed down at all, but it is written *simply*, without all the 50-cent words I used to impress my English teacher all those years ago!

And the result, hopefully, is that the theory and practical suggestions found in the book sound accessible and understandable. (At least, that's my goal.)

It may take some practice, but eventually, writing like you speak will become second nature.

Exercise #20 – Write Like You Speak
1. Using the plans you made in the previous two exercises, start tackling the creation of your next piece of content. For simplicity sake, let's make this a written piece, perhaps a blog post or short article for placement in an online article bank or for social media.
2. Follow the "write like you speak" method of outlining

your points, then talking them out for a few minutes before attempting to duplicate those phrases on paper.

3. Don't be too concerned with how good or bad it turns out, this is just a first draft and we'll be sprucing it up as we move along.

4. Read the next chapter.

25 LIMIT OR ELIMINATE JARGON

The next important step as you're writing this piece of content is to avoid a trap many professionals-turned-content marketers fall into.

Every company, industry and profession has its own virtual dictionary of terms outsiders have little or no use for. "Insiders," though, use these terms regularly, even affectionately.

The more technical the subject of your project is, or the more your audience is limited to "insiders," the greater the likelihood you're going to fall into the use of jargon.

And, this is natural. Especially since the last chapter encouraged you to write like you speak, and if you're neck-deep in your industry and you're constantly surrounded by people who share your insider knowledge, than "like you speak" may include tons of industry jargon.

Why do you do it?

You'll notice this step is not simply "Eliminate Jargon," since this is not only impossible, but may even be detrimental to your content.

But, limiting the amount of jargon you infuse into your copy is very important, especially if your audience includes any who may not be familiar with the words you're using.

Depending on the audience and the purpose of what you're writing, you may decide that some use of jargon, perhaps even a lot of it, is justified. Maybe it even adds to the power of the message.

If so, go for it.

But, if you can't *completely* justify a jargon-laden message, change it.

How do you do it?

Limiting or eliminating jargon has to start with identifying it.

The most effective way to do so is to run your initial draft past someone who is completely removed from your industry or profession and making note of every word or phrase that trips them up.

Of course, this may not always be practical.

At the very least, review your initial draft word by word and ask yourself, "if I wasn't immersed in this subject every day, would I know what _____ meant?"

If there's any doubt at all, think about how important that particular word or phrase really is to the power of the content, and either eliminate it or clarify it accordingly.

After you've been through this process several times, you'll probably be able to limit or eliminate jargon without thinking too much about it. Just be careful not to slip back into old habits thoughtlessly, or to pick up unnecessary new jargon as it's coined.

Exercise #21 – Limit or Eliminate Jargon

1. Review your draft from Exercise #20
2. If it contains any industry-specific jargon that's not absolutely crucial to the effectiveness of the article, zap it.
3. If the jargon is important enough, add clarifying statements to make sure that anyone not familiar with your industry will still be able to benefit from your content.
4. Read the next chapter.

---

26 TRUST YOUR FIRST DRAFT

If you've been keeping up with the most recent exercises, you should have a rough draft of a blog post or article close at hand that's based on some fairly in-depth market research, audience identification, and pre-planning.

It's written like you speak, and it's free from any unnecessary jargon.

But, frankly, it may still suck.

Warning: Up to this point, you've put a lot of time and effort into preparing and writing this piece. Don't immediately dismiss it as a "first draft" that needs to be crossed-out, crumpled and chucked.

Many people do just that when they finish their first draft. They look at it with a frown on their faces, notice some typos or a sentence they don't like very much, and immediately lose hope in the quality of their work. They immediately decide it's never going to be what they want it to be, so why bother?

Don't let this be you.

Why do you do it?

Remember, in Chapter 23, you got excited about your topic and your audience. You really believed there were benefits to the reader, even to you if you wrote this piece well. Don't let that disappear just because the first draft is less than perfect.

Instead, trust your first draft.

This is the result of your in-depth analysis of the purpose for you're writing in the first place. It's the method you chose to pass along the right information to your audience so they can take the action you wish them to take. It's the result of a lot of effort, and chances are very high it's really, really good.

Really.

You see, your first draft is absolutely saturated with your intuition and – if you wrote it like you speak – your personality. When you immediately rip it apart, those are the first things to go.

And when you're creating content for marketing purposes, those are the very last things you want to remove.

So, does that mean your first draft is perfect? Of course not. Far from it. But perfection is out of reach. You should only be reaching for excellence, and it's no doubt a lot closer to that level.

How do you do it?

This step's simple.

Restrain yourself from crumpling up and throwing out your first draft.

Restrain yourself from pulling apart all your contractions because your internal editor tells you they're "too casual".

Restrain yourself from plugging jargon back in because you're secretly afraid your colleagues will think you're dumb.

Basically, do nothing.

Can you do that?

Exercise #22 – Trust Your First Draft
1. Do nothing. (This should be the easiest exercise in the entire book, but it takes willpower.) 2. Read the next chapter.

27 PROOFREAD

This is where you're going to go over your draft with a fine-toothed comb and make it even better than it already is.

Before you do, though, remember that just last chapter, I asked you to do nothing. That's because your first draft is 80% right.

That's going to be hard for you to accept when you look at it again because we're all our worst critics. Your internal editor has been pointing out everything you've ever done wrong for your entire life, especially when it comes to creative pursuits.

But guess what?

Your internal editor was wrong about whether or not you could be an expert. Your internal editor was also wrong about whether or not that first piece of content you put out there would get any response. (It did, didn't it? You've been monitoring it. Check out the results... Not so bad, right?)

So do me a favor and tell your internal editor to shut up.

Why do we do it?

Now that your internal editor has backed off for a few

minutes, let's keep it real: your first draft has errors.

You're going to trust it to a large extent, but you still need to polish it up before it's ready to do great work for you as a publishable piece of content.

How do we do it?

It's probably not necessary to go back to English class again and relearn all the professional proofreader's marks, or to stock up on red grease pencils.

But, if that makes you more comfortable, go for it.

The point of proofreading at this stage is to eliminate silly errors such as spelling or punctuation. Fix any glaring grammar errors that you didn't purposely put into the piece.

Consider adjusting the formatting if it's not pleasing to the eye, or if, after writing it all down, you decide your initial thoughts on format may have been off the mark.

Another vital step to the proofreading process, if you can manage it, is time.

If a piece is long enough, important enough, or if the audience is large and influential enough, a lot of time may be in order.

Sleep on it, if you can. Allow yourself a day or two before picking it back up again. Look at it with fresh eyes.

If this isn't possible because you're strapped for time, at least take a ten minute break to get up and take your eyes off the words you have worked so hard to produce.

By coming back to them after a break, no matter how long, you're much more likely to notice areas for improvement that you were blind to before.

Exercise #23 – Proofread
1. Glance over the first draft you created in Exercises #20 and #21
2. Correct any obvious spelling, punctuation or grammar errors that harm the piece.
3. Give it anywhere between 10 minutes and two days.
4. Read it again more carefully, with an eye for format and for any simple errors you overlooked the last time.
5. Read the next chapter.

28 READ IT ALOUD

Yes, you'll feel funny doing this. People may look at you strangely; you may even become the topic of conversation at the water cooler. But, the power of this one proofreading skill cannot be understated.

Why do you do it?

Chapter 24 stressed the importance of writing like you speak. How else can you confirm you've hit that all-important bulls-eye without reading the work aloud and feeling how easily it rolls off your tongue?

You can't.

How do you do it?

Listen to the words as you read.

Listen objectively and you'll no doubt pick up on the spots where a phrase trips you up. That's a spot to mark and consider rewording. If it didn't sound right to you – the person who wrote it and supposedly knew what you were trying to say – then it's not going to sound right to a reader coming across it for the first time.

You'll hear the momentary stutter as the brain stumbles over an unclear thought. Mark this on the draft as a place to consider adding clarification or explanation. Or, a spot where the logic of your argument could use some help.

You'll notice the deep breath as the lungs recover from a run-on sentence. Guess what? You need to break that sentence up. Mark it down.

If you apply no other step in this section, making a habit of reading your work aloud will still work wonders with the quality of your content.

Exercise #24 – Read it Aloud
1. Go ahead, do it.
2. Each time something sounds slightly off to your ear, or is difficult to read, mark up the draft to indicate a change may be necessary.
3. Read the next chapter.

29 TRASH YOUR FIRST DRAFT

I can hear you now.

"Wait a minute! Didn't he say I'm supposed to trust my first draft? Isn't it the result of all my hard work? What gives?"

The fact is, Chapters 26 and 29 work together perfectly. This is the yang to Chapter 26's yin. The jelly to Chapter 26's peanut butter...

You get the point.

Right after you finish your first draft, your internal editor would like nothing more than to have you rip it up and throw it out.

But it's worth so much more than that.

So we've given it a fair shake. And we've given it adequate time.

Why do you do it?

When you finish your first draft, you are holding in your hands the written equivalent of a handful of pure coal.

You've recognized it's value: it contains all the elements you need to reach your audience with the information they're interested in, in the manner that works best to accomplish the purpose you have set out for it.

So now you start proofreading.

You put your words under pressure. You give it time. You cut it, you squeeze it some more, and you heat it up again.

Then, you read it aloud. More imperfections are becoming obvious, but you can see its inner beauty shining through. So at this point, you're ruthless. Merciless.

Now's your chance to cut it close and polish it to a brilliant shine.

Now what do you have in your hands? Where you used to have that lump of coal, you now find a gorgeous diamond, ready for display.

The point is, don't fall in love with the functional coal you started with. Sure, it's got value. But when you look at it next to the diamond it can become, it's initial value pales in comparison.

How do you do it?

Take full advantage of the proofreading methods described. Make the necessary changes and polish your words until they reach that level of excellence you're shooting for.

Run through the writing-proofreading-reading aloud cycle as many times as necessary to eliminate every item that jumps out at you.

Exercise #25 – Trash Your First Draft

1. Pull out that first draft you marked up in Exercises #23 and #24.
2. Fix all the errors you noticed, then read it aloud again.
3. Rinse and repeat with extreme prejudice until you're certain this piece of content is as good as you can possibly make it.
4. Read the next chapter.

30 KNOW WHEN TO LET IT GO

Yes, eventually your work will be as good as you can reasonably expect to make it.

Perfect? Of course not.

Excellent? Yes.

And when your work reaches that level, you'll no doubt find the benefits outweigh the extra effort it took to get there.

Exercise #26 – Know When to Let it Go
1. Let it go.
2. Publish it. (See Chapter 18)
3. Read the next chapter.

31 GROWING YOUR TROPICAL DEPRESSION

Remember, this storm is constantly spinning.

It has to, or it's going to peter out.

So there are two cycles going on here that both keep everything in motion:

The Instant Expert Formula:

The cycle of decision making, research, content creation and content distribution was covered in Section Two:

1. **Initial decision making** – figuring out which of the intersecting points from your Disparate Forces is going to be your topic(s) of choice to build your content around.
2. **Finding a niche** – fitting that topic(s) into a marketable niche with an established or identifiable target audience and (possibly) competition.
3. **Narrowing the focus** – positioning yourself within that niche in such a way that you can successfully market to a broad enough audience while handling the competition.
4. **Deciding on the media** – choosing the channels and formats most effective for the content you want to

produce and audience you need to speak to.

5. **Creating your content** – The 10-step Checklist for Creating Killer Content!
6. **Getting published** – distributing that content effectively on your own or via one or more 3rd parties.
7. **Re-evaluating** – monitoring and analyzing the entire process with an eye for efficiency and efficacy; seeing what worked and repeating it, seeing what didn't work and eliminating it.

You're going to keep that cycle going by constantly monitoring the content you create and distribute, and making tiny but meaningful (kaizen) improvements to it with each progressive piece you create.

The 10-step Checklist for Creating Killer Content:

Then, contained in Step 5 of that formula is The 10-step Checklist for Creating Killer Content:

1. **Think About Your Audience** – Targeting your content to solve a problem for your audience.
2. **Plan Ahead** – Creating efficiencies and guaranteeing success.
3. **Get Excited** – Putting your personal best into every piece.
4. **Write Like You Speak** – Making your content conversational and engaging.
5. **Limit or Eliminate Jargon** – Avoid one of the biggest problems rookie content marketers make.
6. **Trust Your First Draft** – It came out this way for a reason, so trust that.
7. **Proofread** – Get the technical junk out of the way.
8. **Read Aloud** – Verify the content is conversational.

9. **Trash Your First Draft** – Get it right the *second* time.
10. **Know When to Let it Go** – Concentrate on excellence, not perfection.

With each piece of content you create, as you complete these 10 steps, you move back to Step 6 of the Instant Expert Formula and move through that cycle again as well.

By combining the synergistic power of these two cycles, your content marketing strategy will progress steadily from a conglomeration of Disparate Forces to a slowly churning Tropical Disturbance, then to a fast-moving Tropical Depression, and finally...

Section Four:
Hurricane

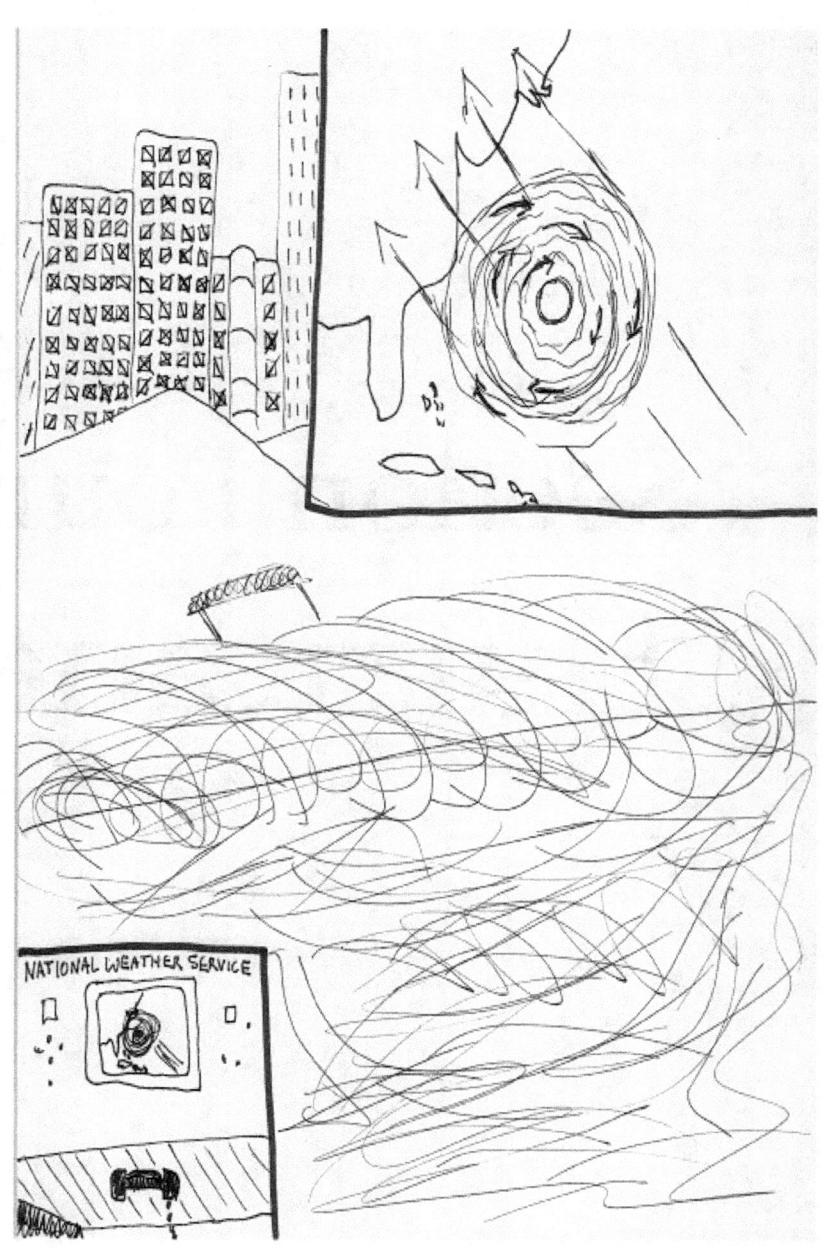

32 PREPARING FOR LANDFALL

When you finally reach the Hurricane stage, your content marketing strategy is operating like a well-oiled machine.

You're spinning through the Instant Expert and Killer Content cycles quickly and efficiently, constantly improving, building strength and power as you go.

You've definitely made a name for yourself at this point, and absolutely everyone (who matters) has taken notice. And a lot of them are already starting to take action!

The eye of the storm

One important benefit you should be experiencing as you enter this stage of your Hurricane's development is the fact that you have work coming in. You're starting to profit from all that hard work you've put in.

As a real hurricane progresses from a tropical depression to a tropical cyclone, the eye – a relatively calm circle in the center of that chaotic storm – grows to potentially miles across.

As the storm passes over land and water, the calm at the eye of the storm provides an incredible contrast to the fury of the storm surrounding that eye.

In Content Marketing Hurricane terms, that central eye is where you do your work.

You see, all the furious effort you've put into building your Content Marketing Hurricane has combined to create a powerful marketing machine that is constantly out there in the world spreading your name and your message near and far, sucking in prospects and leads, and building your reputation for you.

Meanwhile, in the calm at the center of that storm, you're closing deals and getting paid.

If it's done right, it's truly a beautiful thing.

Time for advanced basics

Now that your strategy is transitioning into a full-fledged Hurricane, it's time to head out and take another glance at the big picture.

You're not just working on one piece of content at a time any more, and you're not just experimenting with publication.

Instead, you're turning into a media mogul in charge of Brand You, and that means you need to take some time to think about what you've really been building here.

To that end, let's go over some things I like to call "advanced basics". In other words, this is stuff you probably know, but that's easy to forget in the day-to-day fury of keeping the storm spinning.

Remember, you're heading for landfall here. There are a lot of members of your target audience living on the coast, and they're watching your Hurricane heading right for them.

It would be a real shame to let it all fall apart just before you get there because you forgot what you were really doing.

What is content marketing?

Content marketing means different things to different people, because out of necessity, it has to be customized to each individual, organization or industry that uses it.

But, for the sake of our discussion, I'm going to go with the following general definition:

> *Content marketing is the consistent, strategic production of <u>valuable</u> information, through media your current or potential customers <u>enjoy</u> consuming, in order to help them know, like and trust you, viewing you as a valued source of help at the <u>right time</u>.*

A few points that I underlined in the above definition bear some quick elaboration:

- **Valuable** – Content marketing is not about throwing together a few paragraphs of meaningless junk, stuffed full of keywords for the Google robots and telling people something they already know. That's called wasting time. The kind of content we're talking about here is information you could easily sell, but choose instead to share freely. Information your customer values.
- **Enjoyable** – To have true value, your customer needs to enjoy taking in your content. This means a few

things: first, you need to understand your customer and figure out what type of message she'll get the most out of. But also, since everyone learns and engages with information differently, this dictates the variety of different types of content you're going to need to consider creating if you want to reach your target audience effectively.

- **Timely** – One of the most difficult, but rewarding, aspects of good content marketing is its consistency. Producing high-quality content on a consistent basis isn't easy. Distributing it effectively and working to engage your audience wherever your content goes isn't easy either. But it's a blast! And it's how you're going to manage to strike the right chord with the right person at the right time, bringing the reward back to you.

Keep this definition in mind at all times.

Print it out and post it above your desk. Repeat it five times every morning.

If you forget what you're doing when you're marketing with content, your powerful Content Marketing Hurricane will end up more like a pile of manure hitting a fan.

Why is it so important?

Marketing has changed dramatically in the last few decades.

At this point, businesses are going to sink or swim based on their ability to successfully implement a good content marketing strategy.

Small or independent businesses, traditionally the backbone of most free market economies, are in the very best position to leverage the power of content marketing to further level the playing field in their industries.

Here are a few huge benefits your small business can experience if you're doing content marketing right:

- **Search Engine Ranking** – By consistently adding quality content to your web presence, whether it be in the form of blog posts, landing pages, social media conversation, online video or podcasts, you're creating two things Google absolutely loves: relevant information their audience will appreciate, and links that connect your content to other sources of relevant information their audience will appreciate. But, it has to be written correctly and distributed properly to accomplish this vital purpose.
- **Expert Status** – Loads of free, valuable content, distributed widely and ranking high in the search engines, creates a certain aura about you. Your name becomes synonymous with quality information about your subjects of choice, so you become the go-to-person or company in peoples' minds. Soon, your audience will be seeking you out when they have questions or concerns about your subject, and that's where the tires meet the road.
- **Inbound Marketing** – Well-planned and strategic content marketing is a huge part of an inbound marketing plan. Unlike old-style interruptive marketing (such as telemarketing calls at dinner time, pop-up windows on websites or TV ads) inbound marketing relies on broadcasting information that your target audience (your hottest prospects) want to consume and share with other like-minded people. This way, when you're ready to offer something for sale to your prospects, they don't need to get over the

initial "who is this and why are they trying to sell me" phase that always accompanies a telemarketing call or advertisement.

Always remember the inherent value of content marketing, especially when you're crunched for time and have to choose between polishing up that next blog post or going to bed early.

It's simply the way of the world these days. If you're not marketing with content, you're falling behind.

So it pays to do it, and it pays (even better) to do it right.

How much? How soon? How often?

The short answer is... it depends.

Every strategy is different as it fills different needs and targets different people.

But the bottom line fact is, it's not quick and it's not necessarily easy. To be truly effective, it's going to take a lot of content, distributed far and wide as often as possible. So you're best off starting as soon as you possibly can.

This entire book has been about creating the foundation for a successful content marketing strategy, but if I had to sum up the "next steps" you'll need to take after successfully implementing all the suggestions in this book, I'd say this:

"Create as much quality content as you possibly can and spread it as far as you possibly can, right now!"

Because the Internet is just getting bigger while your

audience's attention span gets smaller. You have no time to lose.

How do you get started?

The more research you do online about the subject of content marketing, the more conflicting information you'll find. I'm not going to sit here and tell you my methods are the only way to succeed, or even the right way for you.

As I said at the beginning of the book, I'm not promising you anything, because this industry changes on a dime.

But, since it's worked well for me so far, I'll let you know how I would do it if I were starting from scratch tomorrow.

Brainstorming

Here are a few questions I'd ask myself:

- Who is my target audience?
- What do they want and need to know about my area of expertise?
- How far can I narrow down my subject while still having plenty to say?
- What valuable information would people likely be willing to pay for?
- And how can I best offer it to them free?

The answers to these questions should give me a starting point for brainstorming content ideas. I would sit down for an hour or two and generate a minimum of 100 ideas that would appeal to my target audience, and can be communicated in ways my target audience will appreciate.

For each of the ideas I come up with, I'd try to quickly outline two or three main points I want to cover under that topic.

Then, I'd think about which content format might be most appropriate for each subject I've written down.

Many will work well as textual blog posts. Others may do better as videos, or presentations. Some may include audio, such as interviews with other experts. Many will be able to be re-purposed in multiple formats, which works even better.

Editorial Calendar

Next, I'd need to be brutally honest with myself:

- What schedule can I commit to for creating content regularly?
- What can I commit to doing to distribute and promote my content?
- How long can I realistically keep up the schedule I'm arranging?

These were tough questions to answer truthfully, especially when I was just starting out. But now I'm not surprised at the amount of time it takes to make this happen.

Of course, it could be different for you.

Reading this book and completing the 25 exercises it contains helped, I hope.

But, unless words flow fast and smooth from your mind to your fingertips, and you know social media like the back of your hand, you're probably going to find the entire blogging/syndicating/retweeting thing a bit overwhelming.

Unfortunately, as I mentioned above, many would-be success stories have never occurred because the hopeful content marketers got caught up in one thing or another and found they were unable or unwilling to stick to their content creation schedule.

I'll stress again, it's not easy. But it's so worth it.

Once I had a realistic idea in mind and in writing as to how much content I could produce and how often, I'd set up an official editorial calendar.

You can do this on any paper or on-screen calendar program you like, as long as it's something you plan to keep in front of you at all times.

This becomes your Bible, where you look for guidance when times get hard.

I'd insert my 100 or more ideas for blog posts, videos, podcasts, etc. into the calendar on the days I want to publish them over the course of the next several months, making sure to build in time for plenty of research and rewriting.

Then, I'd buckle down and start pounding out the content using the Instant Expert and Killer Content cycles we went over in Sections Two and Three.

Strategy

This whole book has been about strategy to some extent, but of course I've barely scratched the surface when it comes to the more advanced strategy details you'll eventually want to know.

A lot of those details will come to you through experience, but for more inspiration and information on the subject than I could ever provide you, I've included a Recommended Reading section at the back of the book that includes some great books on strategy.

But, before we wrap this thing up, here are a few items to consider as you begin working your way through your editorial calendar:

- Although each individual piece of content is valuable in itself, "the hurricane" can't build up speed and intensity unless each piece builds on the last. That doesn't mean each piece needs to directly connect like an ongoing series but rather that each piece needs to work together with a cohesive theme and recognizable voice so people can start putting things together in their minds.
- Different kinds of messages lend themselves to different kinds of media. So, although a particular topic may work very well in a 750-word blog post, if you're going to re-purpose that content to make a video, reading the blog post into the camera is NOT going to work. Experiment with the different methods and media until you find the right mix that works well for you and your audience, then focus on what works.
- Always keep your goals in mind. If you are using content marketing to eventually sell a product or service to a group of people who have shown themselves to be hot prospects for that sale, make sure your content production is heading toward that goal. It would be foolish to try to sell them on every piece of content. As a matter of fact, that would be disastrous to your content marketing strategy. But at the same

time, it's possible to get so caught up in the production of valuable content that you never get around to a call-to-action. Remember that you're not looking for readers, you're looking for customers.

- Social Media (such as Facebook, Twitter, LinkedIn and Google+) is a fantastic tool for getting your content out there in front of your audience, sharing what you're doing and starting conversations about it. But, it's also a huge time waster if you're not careful. You absolutely MUST take advantage of this technology to quickly and economically distribute your content and build relationships with your audience. But don't get so caught up in it your content creation or the other work your content is intended to market begins to suffer.

- Finally, remember that your strategy is fluid and will need to change as circumstances change and feedback comes in. Don't stubbornly stick to a plan that's not working. Test, test, test. And change as needed to take advantage of the information you receive.

Above all, have fun.

I know I've said it before, but it's worth repeating: If you're not having fun, your audience can tell, and they're not going to have much fun either.

Now let's wrap things up with the last two short chapters: a lesson in what NOT to do, and what TO do.

33 THE TORNADO

If you've ever been in the path of a tornado, you know how powerful they can be.

It's one of Mother Nature's most destructive forces, and the sight of that funnel cloud can strike the fear of God into the heart of the bravest cowboy.

But one of the scariest things about tornadoes is their rarity and their unpredictability.

You never know where or when one is going to show up.

You don't know how long it'll stick around.

You have no idea how strong it will be, what direction it's going to move, or whether it's going to destroy your trailer or Aunt Jessie's next door.

You just don't know.

The Content Marketing Tornado

Please, don't create a Content Marketing Tornado.

If you have something worth saying, and a target audience

who wants to hear it, then give them the courtesy of being consistent and professional.

Don't come out of a blue sky with a 300 page e-book touting yourself as the world's #1 expert on organic green tea farming, blitz the heck out of the social media channels with ads for your book, and then disappear just as quickly.

While you're sitting home, shaking your head and wondering why no one bought your book, the rest of the world's green tea lovers are wondering just what the heck all that was about!

They didn't know you, they didn't like you, they certainly didn't trust you. And buying your book was not a priority.

You blew in like a tornado, hopped around in their trailer park, did some damage, then disappeared.

And good riddance.

34 THE HURRICANE!

Instead, if there's anything you bring home from this book, let it be this:

Stay consistent. Build up slowly. Give everyone a chance to see you coming, feel the wind in their face, and smell the ozone before you force them to take cover.

Respect the industry and respect your audience. Respect those folks who are out there with you building their own Content Marketing Hurricanes.

And when you finally make landfall, appreciate it. And give a little something back if you can.

Because what, really, is a Hurricane if there's no one around to appreciate it's awesome power?

In the immortal words of William Shakespeare: "it is a tale told by an idiot, full of sound and fury, signifying nothing."

ABOUT THE AUTHOR

Justin P Lambert is a content marketing specialist living and working in Hickory, North Carolina. He owns and operates Words That Begin With You, a content marketing agency focused primarily on small- to medium-size businesses and startups.

If you'd like to discuss creating a Content Marketing Hurricane in your own organization, Justin provides marketing consultation, content strategy and content creation services. The initial "getting to know you" phone call or e-mail is always free, and you can just mention reading The Content Marketing Hurricane to get 25% off your first project with Words That Begin With You!

Connect with Justin:

Twitter: http://www.twitter.com/justinplambert

Facebook: http://www.facebook.com/justinplambertwrites

Google+: http://bit.ly/182U3qZ

LinkedIn: http://www.linkedin.com/company/words-that-begin-with-you/

Blog: http://www.justinplambert.net/blog

APPENDIX A

RECOMMENDED READING

Here, in no particular order, are some really fantastic books and blogs you should read to get far more information about content marketing, content marketing strategy, and related topics.

BLOGS
The Content Marketing Institute
I'm probably safe in saying these folks started  it all, including the Godfather of Content Marketing, Joe Pulizzi. That being said, the CMI blog has probably taught me more than any other single source about the industry I'm proud to call my own.

Sprout Content
I've had the opportunity to  work with Debbie and Dechay many times and I consider Sprout to be a model content creation and strategy agency: pleasant, efficient, professional, and very good at what they do. **Special Bonus:** They just wrote a book called Brands in Glass Houses: How to Embrace Transparency and Grow Your Business Through Content Marketing . I strongly recommend picking up a copy and checking it out!

Copyblogger

Brian and Simone should probably be listed alongside CMI because, although it wasn't necessarily called content marketing at the  time, they were definitely preaching the selling with content mantra for many years. And to this day, although the blog delves in a number of tangential areas, they're still a strong goto source.

Moz

Moz is a software company that has always based its marketing on providing industry-leading information  about SEO (which their fantastic software assists with.) Excellent information, and a fun mixture of formats and channels that keeps things interesting. I especially like the way they've provided a crowdsourced blog that runs parallel to their corporate blog and allows them to curate the best posts from that blog to place on their own as well. Great idea.

Convince and Convert

Jay Baer has done an  awesome job focusing what can be a too-broad subject. His personal insights are always killer, and he attracts fantastic guest bloggers too. But actually, my favorite resource from C&C is their "One Thing" e-mail newsletter which offers up one golden curated article a day that always manages to grab my attention. **Special Bonus:** Jay also has a new book just out called Youtility: Why Smart Marketing Is about Help Not Hype . I haven't had the opportunity to read it yet, but it's on my list, and I'm sure it'll be great.

Hubspot

Hubspot is another software producer whose product makes

199

it easier for businesses to take advantage of the benefits of inbound and content marketing. So, in their own content marketing efforts, they provide an ongoing case study. They are prolific, creative, and engaging across the board. I can't count how many times I've filled out a form to download a new resource from Hubspot. It must be dozens. Great stuff.

Contently (The Content Strategist)
The Content Strategist is
one of the most
consistently worthwhile
reads I've come across.
 I've worked pretty extensively with Contently as one of their writers-for-hire and have nothing but rave reviews on that side of things as well. But the blog is fantastic. And their new incorporation of video is just stellar too.

BOOKS

There's really too many to list here and do them justice. So, I've included all of them in a Recommended Reading page on my website, and I encourage you to come check it out: http://www.justinplambert.net/recommended-reading